Bond
No.1 for exam success

Verbal Reasoning

Assessment Papers

8–9 years

OXFORD
UNIVERSITY PRESS

OXFORD
UNIVERSITY PRESS

Great Clarendon Street, Oxford, OX2 6DP, United Kingdom

Oxford University Press is a department of the University of Oxford.
It furthers the University's objective of excellence in research,
scholarship, and education by publishing worldwide. Oxford is
a registered trade mark of Oxford University Press in the UK and in
certain other countries

British Library Cataloguing in Publication Data
Data available

978-0-19-277991-5

10 9 8 7 6 5 4 3 2 1

Paper used in the production of this book is a natural, recyclable
product made from wood grown in sustainable forests.
The manufacturing process conforms to the environmental
regulations of the country of origin.

Printed in China

Acknowledgements

The publishers would like to thank the following for permissions to
use copyright material:

Page make-up: OKS Prepress, India
Cover illustrations: Lo Cole

Although we have made every effort to trace and contact all
copyright holders before publication this has not been possible in all
cases. If notified, the publisher will rectify any errors or omissions at
the earliest opportunity.

Links to third party websites are provided by Oxford in good faith
and for information only. Oxford disclaims any responsibility for
the materials contained in any third party website referenced in
this work.

Before you get started

What is Bond?

This book is part of the Bond Assessment Papers series for verbal reasoning, which provides a **thorough and continuous course in verbal reasoning** from ages six to twelve. It builds up verbal reasoning skills from book to book over the course of the series.

What does this book cover?

Verbal reasoning questions can be grouped into four distinct groups: sorting words, selecting words, anagrams, coded sequences and logic. This book practises a wide range of questions appropriate to the age group drawn from all these categories. One of the key features of Bond Assessment Papers is that each one practises **a very wide variety of skills and question types** so that children are always challenged to think – and don't get bored repeating the same question type again and again. We believe that variety is the key to effective learning. It helps children 'think on their feet' and cope with the unexpected.

The age given on the cover is for guidance only. As the papers are designed to be reasonably challenging for the age group, any one child may naturally find him or herself working above or below the stated age. The important thing is that children are always encouraged by their performance. Working at the right level is the key to this.

What does the book contain?

- **20 papers** – each one contains 45 questions.
- **Scoring devices** – there are score boxes next to the questions and a Progress Chart at the back. The chart is a visual and motivating way for children to see how they are doing. Encouraging them to colour in the chart as they go along and to try to beat their last score can be highly effective!
- **Next Steps Planner** – advice on what to do after finishing the papers can be found on the inside back cover.
- **Answers** – located in an easily-removed central pull-out section.

How can you use this book?

One of the great strengths of Bond Assessment Papers is their flexibility. They can be used at home, school and by tutors to:

- provide regular verbal reasoning practice in **bite-sized chunks**
- **highlight strengths and weaknesses** in the core skills
- identify **individual needs**
- set **homework**
- set **timed formal practice tests** – allow about 30 minutes.

It is best to start at the beginning and work through the papers in order.

What does a score mean and how can it be improved?

If children colour in the Progress Chart at the back, this will give an idea of how they are doing. The Next Steps Planner inside the back cover will help you to decide what to do next to help a child progress. We suggest that it is always valuable to go over any wrong answers with children.

Don't forget the website…!

Visit www.assessmentpapers.co.uk for lots of advice, information and suggestions on everything to do with Bond, helping children to do their best, and exams.

Paper 1

Underline the pair of words most similar in meaning.

Example   come, go   <u>roam, wander</u>   fear, fare

1 alley, lane   real, false   back, forward

2 good, bad   bake, oven   heavy, weighty

3 beat, lose   bite, nip   bath, room

4 nose, face   shallow, river   correct, right

5 come, go   sorry, glad   closed, shut

5

Find the three-letter word which can be added to the letters in capitals to make a new word. The new word will complete the sentence sensibly.

Example   The cat sprang onto the MO.   <u>USE</u>

6 SN days make a week.   _____

7 We put SS on our feet.   _____

8 He FED his cup to the brim.   _____

9 They SED me the way to the town.   _____

10 I would like to hear a story BEE I go to sleep.   _____

5

Underline two words, one from each group, that go together to form a new word. The word in the first group always comes first.

Example   (hand, <u>green</u>, for)   (light, <u>house</u>, sure)

11 (is, be, it)   (bed, low, high)

12 (shut, open, in)   (side, back, air)

13 (for, form, fear)   (car, got, back)

14 (toe, finger, hand)   (rip, tip, side)

15 (face, hair, hand)   (shave, some, were)

5

(1)

Change the first word of the third pair in the same way as the other pairs to give a new word.

Example   bind, hind   bare, hare   but, <u>hut</u>

16   art, part   ale, pale   ant, _____

17   ill, till   all, tall   ear, _____

18   pick, prick   feed, freed   tied, _____

19   ran, rain   man, main   pan _____

20   top, stop   tar, star   tab, _____   ◯ 5

Fill in the missing letters. The alphabet has been written out to help you.

A B C D   E   F   G   H   I J K L M N O P Q R S T U V W X Y Z

Example   AB is to CD as PQ is to <u>RS</u>.

21   A is to D as G is to _____.

22   3B is to 4D as 5F is to _____.

23   ABD is to BCE as CDF is to _____.

24   MAB is to NBC as OCD is to _____.

25   9AB is to 8CD as 7EF is to _____.   ◯ 5

Fill in the crosswords so that all the given words are included. You have been given one letter as a clue in each crossword.

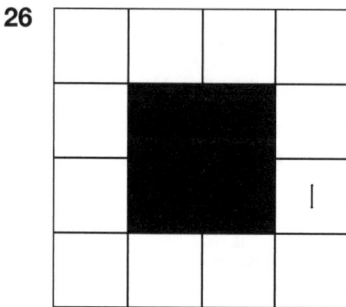

26

27

edit, hint, home, tent   ends, moss, term, time

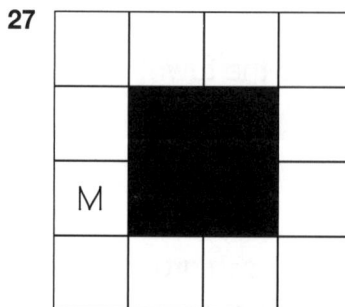

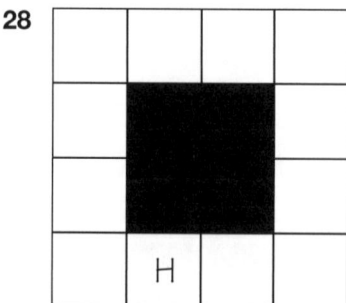

28

heap, ship, wags, wish   ◯ 3

Fill in the missing number in each sequence.

    Example   2   4   6   8   <u>10</u>

29   12   15   _____   21   24

30   1996   1998   _____   2002   2004

31   20   17   14   11   _____

32   4.5   5.0   5.5   6.0   _____

33   19   _____   22   25   29

34   20   18   15   11   _____

6

If the code for PEARS is 13579, what are the codes for the following words?

35   ARE   _____   **36**   RAP   _____

37   SPA   _____   **38**   SEE   _____

39   PEA   _____

What do these codes stand for?

40   91357 _____   **41**   511357   _____

7

Here are some TV programmes.

> 14:00   Play School
>
> 14:15   Cartoons
>
> 15:30   Think Twice
>
> 16:00   The School on the Hill
>
> 16:30   News

How many minutes do these programmes last?

42   Play School   __ minutes   **43**   Cartoons   __ minutes

44   Think Twice   __ minutes   **45**   The School on the Hill   __ minutes

4

Now go to the Progress Chart to record your score!   Total   **45**

Paper 2

Underline the word in brackets closest in meaning to the word in capitals.

Example   UNHAPPY (unkind death laughter <u>sad</u> friendly)

1 CLEVER   (school bright pupil stupid trick)

2 QUICK   (slow fast speed walk step)

3 LAUGH   (cry taught funny chuckle humour)

4 MODERN   (easy today young new trend)

5 SIMPLE   (crazy silly hard easy straight)

5

Find the missing number by using the two numbers outside the brackets in the same way as the other sets of numbers.

Example   2 [8] 4   3 [18] 6   5 [<u>25</u>] 5

6 3 [9] 6   4 [6] 2   1 [__] 6

7 5 [10] 2   4 [12] 3   6 [__] 2

8 2 [5] 3   7 [8] 1   2 [__] 8

9 7 [6] 1   5 [3] 2   8 [__] 4

10 15 [5] 3   21 [3] 7   16 [__] 4

5

Find the letter which will end the first word and start the second word.

Example   peac (<u>h</u>) ome

11 han (__) oor

12 mat (__) ver

13 sal (__) ill

14 duc (__) ite

15 mas (__) est

5

Fill in the crosswords so that all the given words are included. You have been given one letter as a clue in each crossword.

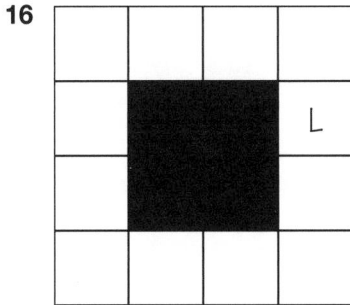

16

	■		L
	■		

cats, camp, plum, sham

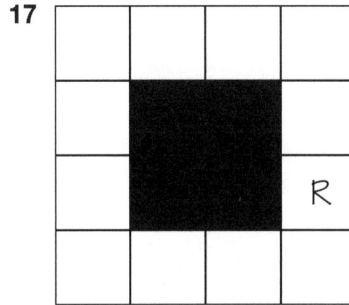

17

	■		
	■		R

beam, bend, dark, milk

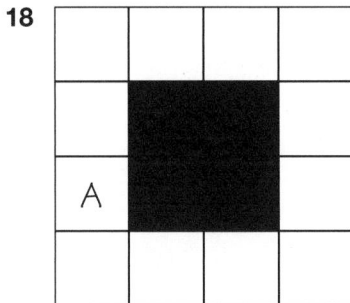

18

	■		
A	■		

bank, bear, king, ring

3

Underline two words, one from each group, that go together to form a new word. The word in the first group always comes first.

Example   (hand, green, for)   (light, house, sure)

19 (bed, for, right)   (tub, cot, side)

20 (near, after, under)   (some, ground, set)

21 (in, an, it)   (left, form, just)

22 (far, near, out)   (law, police, here)

23 (far, for, ran)   (take, give, us)

5

Change the first word into the last word by changing one letter at a time and making a new word in the middle.

Example   CASE CASH LASH

24 PANE   _____   PINK

25 COMB   _____   HOME

26 HOPE _____ COPY

27 HATE _____ MITE

28 COLD _____ GILD

If the code for POSTER is 235689, what are the codes for the following words?

29 STOP _____   **30** SET _____

What do these codes stand for?

31 632 _____   **32** 6355 _____

33 899 _____

Choose the word or phrase that makes each sentence true.

Example A LIBRARY always has (posters, a carpet, <u>books</u>, DVDs, stairs).

34 A HOUSE always has (a garage, curtains, walls, a doorbell, a fence).

35 A LAKE always has (ducks, boats, fish, swans, water).

36 A CITY always has (farms, buildings, an airport, an underground, a river).

37 A KITCHEN always has (a table, chairs, a stove, plants, a radio).

38 A SCHOOL always has (a cafeteria, a nurse, students, a swimming pool, a bus).

Underline the two words which are made from the same letters.

Example TAP PET <u>TEA</u> POT <u>EAT</u>

39 MEAT TIME TUNE TEAM MUST

40 NUT TEN NET TAN NOT

41 TEST STAB LAST LOST SALT

Remove one letter from the word in capitals to leave a new word.
The meaning of the new word is given in the clue.

Example   AUNT   an insect   _ant_

42 FARM   not near   _____

43 HARM   a piece of meat   _____

44 GROUND   shaped like a ball   _____

45 THAN   you get it from sunbathing   _____   (4

Now go to the Progress Chart to record your score!   Total (45

Paper 3

Underline the two words which are the odd ones out in the following groups of words.

Example   black   <u>king</u>   purple   green   <u>house</u>

1 quiet   peaceful   crowd   calm   concert

2 small   short   enlarge   brief   expand

3 sea   harbour   ocean   pier   lake

4 sturdy   weak   strong   healthy   ill

5 walk   swim   stride   dive   march   (5

Find the three-letter word which can be added to the letters in capitals to make a new word. The new word will complete the sentence sensibly.

Example   The cat sprang onto the MO.   <u>USE</u>

6 The weather was W and sunny.   _____

7 He SCHED high and low for the remote control.   _____

8 I've got some nice, new PYAS to wear.   _____

9 My favourite fruit is an APRI.   _____

10 The octopus caught him with its TACLES.   _____   (5

(7)

Which one letter can be added to the front of all of these words to make new words?

Example _c_are _c_at _c_rate _c_all

11 ___late ___lease ___ony ___each

12 ___right ___ig ___all ___ean

13 ___how ___et ___poon ___nake

14 ___elt ___eal ___at ___oan

15 ___hall ___eal ___mall ___nail

5

Add one letter to the word in capital letters to make a new word. The meaning of the new word is given in the clue.

Example PLAN simple _plain_

16 TROT a fish _____

17 NOSE the opposite of silence _____

18 TICK the opposite of thin _____

19 LATE used to put our food on _____

20 SORT different types of games _____

5

Fill in the crosswords so that all the given words are included. You have been given one letter as a clue in each crossword.

21

	■	■	
	■	■	
		E	

keep, mark, mist, trip

22

	■	■	
	■	■	
		T	

date, fire, half, hard

23

E	■	■	
	■	■	

part, pear, ripe, tide

3

Fill in the missing number in each sequence.

Example   2   4   6   8   <u>10</u>

24   3   6   9   ___   15

25   12   10   8   ___   4

26   12   24   ___   48   60

27   21   32   43   ___   65

28   121   232   ___   454   565

5

These words have been written in code, but the codes are not under the right words.

TOO   OUT   TOT   TO   UP

72   722   247   46   727

Write the correct code for each word.

29 TOO   _____   **30** OUT   _____

31 TOT   _____   **32** TO   _____

33 UP   _____

5

If a = 1, b = 2, c = 3, find the sum of:

34 a + b + c = _____   **35** c + 2b = _____

36 2a + 2b = _____

3

Underline the one word which **cannot be made** from the letters of the word in capital letters.

Example   STATIONERY   stones   tyres   ration   <u>nation</u>   noisy

37 CONSIDER   cried   nice   dear   rice   coin

38 LOWEST   low   west   flow   sew   owl

39 TEACHER   eaten   chat   ear   are   crate

40 INSIDE   den   snide   end   dine   need

4

In each line, underline the word that has its letters in alphabetical order.

41 gas   guzzle   grunt   got

42 apple   ant   ask   ale

43 clever   caution   care   cry

44 deal   dint   dream   drink

45 flow   flea   frank   frog

◯ 5

Now go to the Progress Chart to record your score!   Total ◯ 45

Paper 4

Find and underline the two words which need to change places for each sentence to make sense.

Example   She went to <u>letter</u> the <u>write</u>.

1 The tail wagged her dog when she saw the treat.

2 My sister told my mother to finish her homework.

3 I like to read a bed before book.

4 At my birthday cake we ate ice cream and party.

5 My mum takes the office to her bus.

◯ 5

Underline two words, one from each group, that go together to form a new word. The word in the first group always comes first.

Example   (hand, <u>green</u>, for)   (light, <u>house</u>, sure)

6 (wood, light, sea)   (day, tree, weed)

7 (earth, glass, sand)   (sun, castle, rain)

8 (well, work, pail)   (shop, cut, know)

9 (foot, glove, hand)   (knee, head, shake)

10 (under, over, through)   (sky, place, water)

◯ 5

Fill in the crosswords so that all the given words are included. You have been given one letter as a clue in each crossword.

11

A	■	■	
	■	■	

keen, park, port, torn

12

	■	■	
	■	■	
		S	

easy, heal, hole, lazy

◯ 2

Underline one word in the brackets which is most opposite in meaning to the word in capitals.

Example WIDE (broad vague long <u>narrow</u> motorway)

13 HEALTHY (good doctor hospital ill patient)

14 TEACHER (school pupil lesson term tutor)

15 FRIEND (pal mate foe ally neighbour)

16 MANY (more lots few crowd half)

17 WHOLE (entire part some complete full)

◯ 5

Find the three-letter word which can be added to the letters in capitals to make a new word. The new word will complete the sentence sensibly.

Example The cat sprang onto the MO. <u>USE</u>

18 A baby is an INT. ———

19 A baby goes out in a P. ———

20 A baby CLS on the floor. ———

21 A baby plays with a TLE. ———

22 A baby sits in a HIGHCH. ———

◯ 5

Add one letter to the word in capital letters to make a new word. The meaning of the new word is given in the clue.

Example PLAN simple _plain_

23 WAS an insect _____

24 HOP to expect the best _____

25 LOW the opposite of fast _____

26 HAT to stop _____

27 RAN it pours _____

5

Complete the following expressions by underlining the missing word.

Example Frog is to tadpole as swan is to (duckling, baby, cygnet).

28 Sun is to sunk as pin is to (sink, pin, pink).

29 Eye is to see as ear is to (speak, hear, nose).

30 Bed is to bead as led is to (late, lead, deal).

31 Top is to bottom as right is to (correct, under, left).

32 Speak is to talk as consider is to (count, think, moan).

33 Ail is to bail as ill is to (sill, will, bill).

6

34 boy but why she sty

If these words were written backwards, which word would now come first in alphabetical order?

_____

1

These words have been written in code, but the codes are not under the right words.

BE	BEG	BIN	BEGIN	BEE
244	24538	24	245	238

Write the correct code for each word.

35 BE   36 BEG   37 BIN   38 BEE   39 BEGIN

_____   _____   _____   _____   _____

5

If a = 3, b = 2, d = 6, e = 8, f = 10, find the value of:

40 2f − 2a = ___   **41** 2e − 2b = ___   2

Sue and Omar wear yellow tops.

Lee and Omar wear green trousers.

Sue and Jess wear brown trousers.

Jess and Lee wear red tops.

Who wears:

42 a yellow top and brown trousers?   _____

43 a red top and green trousers?   _____

44 a yellow top and green trousers?   _____

45 a red top and brown trousers?   _____   4

Now go to the Progress Chart to record your score!   Total   45

Paper 5

Which one letter can be added to the front of all of these words to make new words.

Example   <u>c</u>are   <u>c</u>at   <u>c</u>rate   <u>c</u>all

1 __arm   __and   __as   __ollow

2 __old   __hill   __loud   __an

3 __read   __ream   __ark   __ome

4 __and   __right   __ear   __each

5 __rim   __ower   __ride   __lant   5

The train was due in at 10:50. It was 10 minutes late.

6 When did it arrive? _____

I left home at 18:15. It took me 20 minutes to walk to the cinema.

7 When did I get there? _____

13

A pudding takes 50 minutes to cook. I want it to be ready for 13:00.

8 When must I put it into the oven? _____

If these words were placed in alphabetical order, which word would come first?

9 Monday   Thursday   Wednesday   Friday   Tuesday _____

10 May   January   March   February   April _____

11 giraffe   elephant   mouse   horse   dog _____

12 plane   helicopter   kite   balloon   rocket _____

Underline one word in the brackets which is most opposite in meaning to the word in capitals.

Example   WIDE   (broad   vague   long   <u>narrow</u>   motorway)

13 WARM   (hot   cold   icy   sun   fine)

14 BLACK   (dark   brown   white   sooty   coal)

15 HIDE   (lost   last   find   secret   conceal)

16 MORE   (less   many   few   lots   plenty)

17 FIRST   (top   bottom   side   last   enough)

Underline two words which are made from the same letters.

Example   TAP   PET   <u>TEA</u>   POT   <u>EAT</u>

18 MAUL   PART   MAKE   TRAM   TRAP

19 AGES   ALES   APES   SAGE   SAND

20 LIMP   LEAP   PEEP   PEAL   PEARL

21 WARN   WARM   WARD   WARP   DRAW

22 LATE   LINT   TALE   TILE   FILE

Remove one letter from the word in capitals to leave a new word. The meaning of the new word is given in the clue.

Example   AUNT   an insect   *ant*

23 ROAD   a stick   _____

24 PINT   something we use when sewing   _____

25 TINT   a metal   _____

26 CODE   a type of fish   _____

27 HARM   part of our body   _____   (5

Underline the number that completes each sequence.

28 4 is to 16 as 16 is to (72, 64, 60)

29 3 is to 12 as 12 is to (24, 36, 48)

30 32 is to 16 as 16 is to (4, 8, 12)

31 55 is to 11 as 60 is to (11, 12, 14)

32 100 is to 50 as 90 is to (55, 40, 45)   (5

These words have been written in code, but the codes are not under the right words.

STOW   SLOW   STEW   LOW   STOLE

9687   96418   9147   9647   147

Write the correct code for each word.

33 STOW   34 SLOW   35 STEW   36 LOW   37 STOLE

_____   _____   _____   _____   _____   (5

Underline the word in the brackets which goes best with the words given outside the brackets.

Example   word, paragraph, sentence   (pen, cap, letter, top, stop)

38 bed, bunk, mattress   (drawer, cold, warm, film, pillow)

39 car, lorry, bicycle   (train, road, bus, speed, track)

40 sheep, cows, chickens   (farm, tractor, shed, pigs, bird)

41 money, cash, notes   (cheque, bank, lesson, coins, save)

42 mat, tiles, carpet   (curtains, rug, kitchen, sofa, stairs)

5

Fill in the crosswords so that all the given words are included. You have been given one letter as a clue in each crossword.

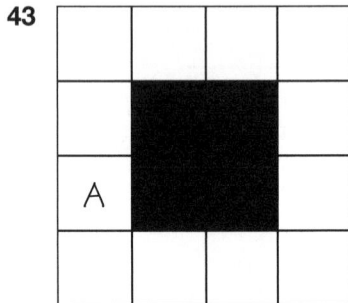

43

lost, rust, tear, tool

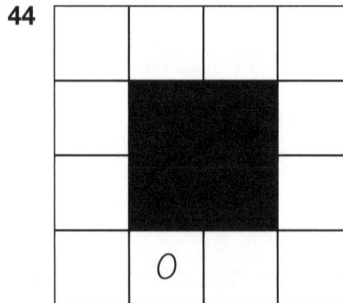

44

leak, sail, shot, took

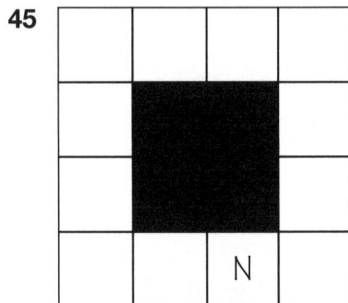

45

less, list, seek, tank

3

Now go to the Progress Chart to record your score!   Total   45

Paper 6

Underline one word in the brackets which is most opposite in meaning to the word in capital letters.

> **Example**   WIDE   (broad   vague   long   <u>narrow</u>   motorway)

1 SHORT   (length   long   low   metre   up)

2 UP   (saw   went   go   down   tall)

3 YOUNG   (old   clothes   pretty   dress   new)

4 EVEN   (smooth   plain   old   odd   straight)

5 FASTEN   (collar   fix   loosen   tie   bind)

5

Fill in the crosswords so that all the given words are included. You have been given one letter as a clue in each crossword.

6

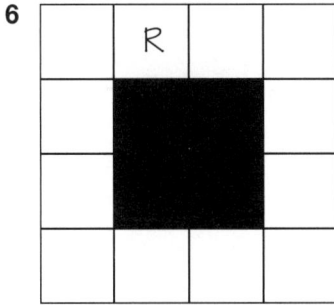

even, idle, iron, noon

7

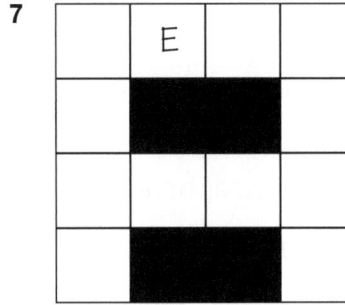

told, nail, want, went

8

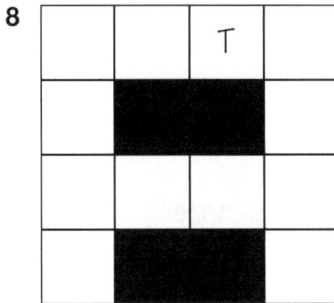

bare, hare, bath, rear

In each line one word has been muddled up. Rearrange the letters so it fits in with the others.

Example   fly spider moth gnat <u>tan</u>   <u>ant</u>

9 dove   lark   wren   tit   low   _____

10 rain   owns mist   hail   fog   _____

11 lump   pear   date   lime   apple   _____

12 cake   pork   wets   buns   ham   _____

13 goat   lamb   deer   loaf   calf   _____

Change the first word into the last word by changing one letter at a time and making a new, different word in the middle.

Example   CASE <u>CASH</u> LASH

14 LAND   _____   PAID

15 PLAN   _____   CLAP

16 PAID   _____   HAIL

17 WAND _____ FIND

18 SILK _____ TILL

Change the first word of the third pair in the same way as the other pairs to give a new word.

Example bind, hind bare, hare but, _hut_

19 rest, test road, toad rent, _____

20 chip, hip park, ark mice, _____

21 tear, tar fear, far bear, _____

22 bet, beat set, seat met, _____

23 and, band old, bold all, _____

In each line, underline the word that has its letters in alphabetical order.

24 ace debt eight more

25 few lips most room

Find the three-letter word which can be added to the letters in capitals to make a new word. The new word will complete the sentence sensibly.

Example The cat sprang onto the MO. _USE_

26 A donkey BS. _____

27 A cock CS. _____

28 A lion RS. _____

29 A dog BS. _____

30 A pig GTS. _____

If the code for LATHER is ABCDEF, what are the codes for the following words?

31 REAL _____ **32** LATE _____ **33** HEAL _____

What do these codes stand for?

34 DEF _____ **35** CEECD _____

18

The day after tomorrow is Friday.

36 What was the day before yesterday? _____

If Joshua was a year older he would be three times as old as his brother. His brother is 4.

37 How old is Joshua? _____

I have 20p more than Gita who has 40p less than Mike. Mike has £1.20.

38 How much does Gita have? _____

39 How much do I have? _____

○ 4

Underline the two words which are the odd ones out in the following groups of words.

Example	black	king	purple	green	house

40 banana   pear   yellow   purple   apple

41 finger   ring   knee   hat   ear

42 rose   daffodil   daisy   leaf   stem

43 tennis   bat   ball   rugby   swimming

○ 4

Fill in the crosswords so that all the given words are included. You have been given one letter as a clue in each crossword.

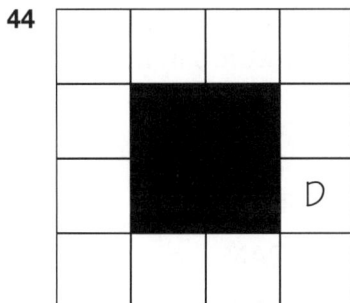

44

ends, laze, lent, tins

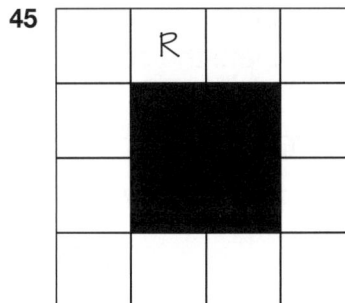

45

bear, ever, gate, grab

○ 2

Look at these groups of words.

Group A Animals   Group B Colours   Group C Birds

Choose the correct group for each of the words below. Write in the letter.

1 purple ___   **2** ferret ___   **3** swan ___   **4** rabbit ___   **5** wren ___   ◯ 5

Underline the pair of words most opposite in meaning.

    Example   cup, mug   coffee, milk   <u>hot, cold</u>

  6   yes, no   tall, fat   roam, wander

  7   happy, glad   teach, learn   blue, sea

  8   sorry, cry   quick, run   less, more

  9   work, play   high, jump   bright, shining

10   rain, puddle   cat, food   wet, dry   ◯ 5

Underline the one word which **cannot be made** from the letters of the word in capital letters.

    Example   STATIONERY   stone   tyres   ration   <u>nation</u>   noisy

11   PROFITS   frost   stiff   spot   soft   sport

12   GROWING   ring   gnaw   grin   wing   iron

13   COWARDS   ward   draws   soars   sword   crow

14   GRAPPLE   pear   rage   leap   gate   grape

15   PATIENT   tape   pint   teen   tent   neat   ◯ 5

Look at the first group of three words. The word in the middle has been made from the other two words. Complete the second group of three words in the same way, making a new word in the middle.

    Example   PAIN   <u>IN</u>TO   <u>TOO</u>K   ALSO   <u>SOON</u>   ONLY

16   CAME   MESH   SHOT   YEAR   _____   CHIN

17   GRIN   GRAB   STAB   PLUM   _____   SCAN

18   MALT   ALSO   SAGO   SMOG   _____   SEAS

19   GATE   GAME   TIME   ROPE   _____   HOSE

20   THIN   MOTH   MOON   STAB   _____   PEGS   ◯ 5

Complete the following sentences by selecting the most sensible word from each group of words given in the brackets. Underline the words selected.

Example The (children, books, foxes) carried the (houses, books, steps) home from the (greengrocer, library, factory).

21 Tom saw a (bird, walrus, rabbit) run down a (chimney, hole, pavement) and into its (drey, burrow, sleep).

22 I feel (cold, lazy, hot) so I must put on a (swim suit, jumper, sandals) – then I will feel warmer in this chilly (sun, wind, day).

23 The (firework, balloons, streamers) were (burst, inflated, candle) to decorate the (room, table, ladder) for the party.

24 Clare (wrote, played, sent) a (page, text, letter) to Anya's mobile (bike, phone, pencil).

25 They (ran, walked, swam) across the (house, class, lake) to the (mist, frog, island).

5

Remove one letter from the word in capital letters to leave a new word. The meaning of the new word is given in the clue.

Example AUNT an insect <u>ant</u>

26 BLESS fewer _____

27 THEN a chicken _____

28 MEAN male _____

29 REED a colour _____

4

Fill in the crosswords so that all the given words are included. You have been given one letter as a clue in each crossword.

30

	■	■	A
	■	■	

host, hymn, note, take

31

■		■	
■	A	■	

ants, arts, open, spar

2

32 If the code for SPIN is ABDE, what is the code for NIPS? _____

33 If the code for RING is CDEF, what is the code for GRIN? _____

34 If the code for SPRIG is ABCDF, what is the code for PRIG? _____

35 If the code for SEAT is 3521, what is the code for TEAS? _____

36 If the code for STEAM is 31526, what is the code for MAST? _____ ⑤

Fill in the missing number or letters in each sequence.

Example 2 4 6 8 <u>10</u>

37	10	20	40	__	160
38	28	24	20	__	12
39	19	25	__	37	43
40	11	__	17	20	23
41	bb	bc	bd	__	bf

⑤

Look at this chart.

	English	Art	Maths	Science	ICT
Boys	4	2	4	6	3
Girls	5	6	2	1	3

42 Which subject is liked by twice as many boys as girls? _____

43 Which subject is three times as popular with girls as with boys? _____

44 Which subject is least popular with girls? _____

45 Which subject was liked equally well by boys and girls? _____ ④

Now go to the Progress Chart to record your score! Total ⑷⑸

Paper 8

If a = 1, b = 2, c = 3, d = 4, e = 5, f = 6, find the sum of:

1 a + b + c = __   **2** d + e + f = __

3 2a + b = __   **4** 2b + c = __

5 3a + 2b = __   **6** e + f = __ ⑥

22

Rearrange the muddled letters in capitals to make a proper word. The answer will complete the sentence sensibly.

Example A BEZAR is an animal with stripes. ZEBRA

7 Half of six is HERET. _____

8 Sheep have a thick OLWO coat. _____

9 Don't drop TILTRE in the street. _____

10 The fire crew used AETRW to put out the blaze. _____

11 The tower of the HRCCHU was floodlit. _____

(5)

Complete the following sentences by selecting the most sensible word from each group of words given in the brackets. Underline the words selected.

Example The (children, books, foxes) carried the (houses, books, steps) home from the (greengrocer, library, factory).

12 It was (hot, cold, freezing) and she (hated, wanted, disliked) a (pie, hot soup, cold drink) to cool her down.

13 Where is my (shoe, coat, book)? I left it (hiding, running, hanging) in the (shelf, kitchen, cupboard).

14 The (king, soldier, dog) sat in his (car, basket, larder) and (swam, growled, argued).

(3)

Underline the pair of words most opposite in meaning.

Example cup, mug   coffee, milk   hot, cold

15 cross, happy   sad, sorry   start, begin

16 neat, tidy   hard, soft   soap, water

17 eat, drink   boil, water   loud, noisy

18 cold, cool   shut, open   oil, tank

19 paper, pencil   pen, write   cry, laugh

(5)

Look at the first group of three words. The word in the middle has been made from the other two words. Complete the second group of three words in the same way, making a new word in the middle.

Example PAIN INTO TOOK   ALSO SOON ONLY

20 RASH   RAIN   GRIN   CLAN   _____   SLIP

21 POST   STAR   ARMY   POSH   _____   INTO

(23)

22	CRAG	CREW	EWES	BLUE	_____	ABLE
23	CHAT	CHIN	RAIN	SLAT	_____	SHAM
24	OVEN	VERY	YOUR	BACK	_____	ETCH

Underline the two words which are the odd ones out in the following groups of words.

Example   black <u>king</u> purple green <u>house</u>

25	cot	sleep	cradle	sing	bed
26	cat	little	water	minute	small
27	road	long	tall	street	fat
28	coat	new	dress	pretty	suit
29	sorry	pleased	happy	glad	old

Fill in the missing letters. The alphabet has been written out to help you.

A B C D E F G H I J K L M N O P Q R S T U V W X Y Z

Example   AB is to CD as PQ is to <u>RS</u>.

30 A30 is to B29 as C28 is to _____.

31 D20 is to E19 as F18 is to _____.

32 100A is to 95B as 90C is to _____.

33 A2 is to B3 as C4 is to _____.

34 F1 is to E2 as D3 is to _____.

Find and underline the two words which need to change places for each sentence to make sense.

Example   She went to <u>letter</u> the <u>write</u>.

35 The drive was parked in the car.

36 We went to holiday for our Scotland.

37 I have to eat my pudding before I can have supper.

38 The shop on my road sweets sells.

39 We are moving our house and selling to Wales.

(24)

If the code for SECOND is ABCDEF, what are the codes for the following words?

40 ONE _____   41 CODE _____   42 ONCE _____

What do these codes stand for?

43 FDEB _____   44 FDAB _____   45 ABEF _____   **6**

Now go to the Progress Chart to record your score!   Total **45**

Paper 9

Underline the pair of words most similar in meaning.

Example   come, go   <u>roam, wander</u>   fear, fare

1 fade, tint   blank, empty   hinder, go

2 cut, slit   hit, miss   less, more

3 dry, fine   rich, poor   tea, coffee

4 add, subtract   hole, gap   red, colour

5 tired, weary   hot, cold   forgot, remember   **5**

Find the three-letter word which can be added to the letters in capitals to make a new word. The new word will complete the sentence sensibly.

Example   The cat sprang onto the MO.   <u>USE</u>

6 The police will FOL the criminal.   _____

7 A DON is sometimes called an ass.   _____

8 Time to stop for a DR of water.   _____

9 He was pleased to go home from HOSAL.   _____

10 You need a BET to carry your shopping in.   _____   **5**

Find the letter which will end the first word and start the second word.

Example   peac (h) ome

11 gat (__) nds   12 non (__) ars   13 min (__) ust

14 ben (__) rim   15 als (__) dds   **5**

(25)

Look at the first group of three words. The word in the middle has been made from the other two words. Complete the second group of three words in the same way, making a new word in the middle.

Example   PAIN   INTO   TOOK   ALSO   <u>SOON</u>   ONLY

16 CLAN   CLOP   STOP   RATS   _____   FISH

17 BAND   BARK   DARK   SLIP   _____   GROW

18 FISH   SHOE   WOES   FAST   _____   TOWN

19 SALT   ALSO   SOOT   PART   _____   CHOP

20 BUSH   BUNK   PINK   STEP   _____   SHOP

⬭ 5

Complete the following sentences by selecting the most sensible word from each group of words given in the brackets. Underline the words selected.

Example   The (<u>children</u>, books, foxes) carried the (houses, <u>books</u>, steps) home from the (greengrocer, <u>library</u>, factory).

21 She spent a (lot, little, some) of money on all the things she had to (buy, sell, gather) for the big (party, card, mess).

22 The (dog, cow, rabbit) barked (kindly, fiercely, slowly) at the (burglars, robbing, scare).

23 Tola (buy, bought, bring) her brother a DVD as a (present, surprised, gifts) for (his, her, my) birthday.

24 Don't (run, walk, stand)! You'll (stop, wait, trip) and hurt your (book, friend, knee).

25 The cinema was (dry, packed, fill) for the premiere of the (pictures, movie, showing) with an all-star (sky, moon, cast).

⬭ 5

If the code for WONDER is 324165, what are the codes for the following words?

26 END _____   27 DEW _____

What do these codes stand for?

28 324 _____   29 3564 _____   30 246 _____

⬭ 5

If a = 1, b = 2, c = 3, d = 4, e = 5, find the sum of:

31 c + d + b = __   32 2a + 2 = __   33 2c + 2d = __

⬭ 3

It takes 1 hour 30 minutes to do the journey. Fill in the missing times.

34–37

Southby (depart)	Eastby (arrive)
_____	12:00
14:30	_____
16:10	_____
_____	18:30

4

If the letters in the following words are arranged in alphabetical order, which letter comes in the middle?

38 FAIRY _____   39 PLACE _____

40 LIGHT _____   41 TEACH _____

4

Worzles and Dingbats like to eat leaves and shoots.

Sninks and Dingbats like snails and slugs.

Worzles and Wigglers like weeds and grass.

Wigglers and Sninks like flies and berries.

42 Who likes berries but not weeds?   _____

43 Who likes leaves, shoots and slugs?   _____

44 Who likes snails and flies?   _____

45 Who likes weeds, grass, flies and berries?   _____

4

Now go to the Progress Chart to record your score!   Total   **45**

Paper 10

Underline the two words which are the odd ones out in the following groups of words.

Example   black   <u>king</u>   purple   green   <u>house</u>

1 child   wash   clean   parent   bath

2 circle   newspaper   ring   hoop   comic

27

3	grey	yellow	apple	blue	cherry
4	jeans	turban	white	brown	sweater
5	bench	arm	seat	chair	leg

(5)

Find the three-letter word which can be added to the letters in capitals to make a new word. The new word will complete the sentence sensibly.

Example The cat sprang onto the MO. <u>USE</u>

6 The CH he sat on was hard. _____

7 The CSE of the river was long and winding. _____

8 The show INS at eight o'clock. _____

9 At the start of the play the ORS appeared on the stage. _____

10 The BN and white dog ran wildly after the ball. _____

(5)

Find the letter which will end the first word and start the second word.

Example peac (<u>h</u>) ome

11 lan (__) are   **12** fea (__) ule

13 gon (__) ver   **14** sto (__) ond

15 cla (__) hite

(5)

These words have been written in code, but the codes are not under the right words.

AT	THE	CHAT	HAT	ACT
2315	15	125	534	315

Write the correct code for each word.

16 AT   **17** THE   **18** CHAT

_____   _____   _____

19 HAT   **20** ACT

_____   _____

(5)

28

Paper 1 (pages 1–3)

1 **alley, lane** Both words mean a type of path or narrow road.
2 **heavy, weighty** Both words mean bulky or big.
3 **bite, nip** Both words mean to snap at or pinch with teeth.
4 **correct, right** Both words mean accurate or exact.
5 **closed, shut** Both words mean fastened or secure.
6 **EVE** seven
7 **HOE** shoes
8 **ILL** filled
9 **HOW** showed
10 **FOR** before
11 **below**
12 **inside**
13 **forgot**
14 **fingertip**
15 **handsome**
16 **pant** The pattern is to put 'p' in front of the first word.
17 **tear** The pattern is to put 't' in front of the first word.
18 **tried** The pattern is to put 'r' after the first letter in the first word.
19 **pain** The pattern is to insert 'i' after the second letter in the first word.
20 **stab** The pattern is to put 's' in front of the first word.
21 **J** The letters move forwards by three letters.
22 **6H** The numbers increase by 1 each time. The letters move forwards by two letters.
23 **DEG** All the letters move forwards by one letter.
24 **PDE** All the letters move forwards by one letter.
25 **6GH** The numbers decrease by 1 each time. All the letters move forwards by two letters.

26

H	O	M	E
I	■	■	D
N	■	■	I
T	E	N	T

27

T	E	R	M
I	■	■	O
M	■	■	S
E	N	D	S

28

W	I	S	H
A	■	■	E
G	■	■	A
S	H	I	P

29 **18** The numbers increase by 3 each time.
30 **2000** The numbers increase by 2 each time.
31 **8** The numbers decrease by 3 each time.
32 **6.5** The numbers increase by 0.5 each time.
33 **20** The number added increases by 1 each time: +1, +2, +3, +4
34 **6** The number subtracted decreases by 1 each time: −2, −3, −4, −5
35 **573** A = 5, R = 7, E = 3
36 **751** R = 7, A = 5, P = 1
37 **915** S = 9, P = 1, A = 5
38 **933** S = 9, E = 3, E = 3
39 **135** P = 1, E = 3, A = 5
40 **SPEAR** 9 = S, 1 = P, 3 = E, 5 = A, 7 = R
41 **APPEAR** 5 = A, 1 = P, 1 = P, 3 = E, 5 = A, 7 = R
42 **15 minutes** From 14:00 to 14:15 is 15 minutes.
43 **75 minutes** From 14:15 to 15:30 is 75 minutes.
44 **30 minutes** From 15:30 to 16:00 is 30 minutes.
45 **30 minutes** From 16:00 to 16:30 is 30 minutes.

Paper 2 (pages 4–7)

1–5 A word that has the same or similar meaning to another word is called a synonym. For example, 'gigantic' is a synonym of 'large'.
1 **bright** 'Clever' and 'bright' are both synonyms meaning intelligent.
2 **fast** 'Quick' and 'fast' are both synonyms meaning speedy.
3 **chuckle** 'Laugh' and 'chuckle' are both sounds showing amusement.
4 **new** 'Modern' and 'new' are both synonyms meaning up to date, fresh.
5 **easy** 'Simple' and 'easy' are both synonyms meaning straightforward.
6–10 Solve these questions by looking at the first set of three and working out how the first and last numbers have been used to arrive at the middle number. Apply this to the second set of three and see if it works. If it does, apply it to the last set.
6 **7** 3 + 6 = 9 and 4 + 2 = 6 so 1 + 6 = 7
7 **12** 5 × 2 = 10 and 4 × 3 = 12 so 6 × 2 = 12
8 **10** 2 + 3 = 5 and 7 + 1 = 8 so 2 + 8 = 10
9 **4** 7 − 1 = 6 and 5 − 2 = 3 so 8 − 4 = 4
10 **4** 15 ÷ 3 = 5 and 21 ÷ 7 = 3 so 16 ÷ 4 = 4
11 **d** hand, door
12 **e** mate, ever
13 **t** salt, till
14 **k** duck, kite
15 **t** mast, test

16

C	A	M	P
A	■	■	L
T	■	■	U
S	H	A	M

17

B	E	N	D
E	■	■	A
A	■	■	R
M	I	L	K

18

B	A	N	K
E	■	■	I
A	■	■	N
R	I	N	G

19 **bedside**	20 **underground**
21 **inform**	22 **outlaw**
23 **forgive**	24 **PINE**
25 **COME**	26 **COPE**
27 **MATE**	28 **GOLD**

29 **5632** S = 5, T = 6, O = 3, P = 2
30 **586** S = 5, E = 8, T = 6
31 **TOP** 6 = T, 3 = O, 2 = P
32 **TOSS** 6 = T, 3 = O, 5 = S, 5 = S
33 **ERR** 8 = E, 9 = R, 9 = R
34 **walls** A 'house' must have 'walls' to be a house. It may or may not have the other things.
35 **water** A 'lake' consists of 'water'. It must have this. It may or may not have the other things.
36 **buildings** A 'city' consists of lots of 'buildings'. It must have these. It may or may not have the other things.
37 **a stove** A 'kitchen' is a place where food is prepared and cooked. Of all the words mentioned, 'a stove' is the word that connects it to a 'kitchen'.
38 **students** A 'school' is where 'students' study. It must have these. It may or may not have the other things.

39 **MEAT, TEAM**	40 **TEN, NET**
41 **LAST, SALT**	
42 **far**	43 **ham**
44 **round**	45 **tan**

Paper 3 (pages 7–10)

1 **crowd, concert** All the other words mean tranquil.
2 **enlarge, expand** All the other words mean 'not very long'.
3 **harbour, pier** All the other words are bodies of water.
4 **weak, ill** All the other words mean fit or well.
5 **swim, dive** All the other words are actions you do out of the water.

6 **ARM** warm	7 **EAR** searched
8 **JAM** pyjamas	9 **COT** apricot
10 **TEN** tentacles	

11 **p** plate, please, pony, peach
12 **b** bright, big, ball, bean
13 **s** show, set, spoon, snake
14 **m** melt, meal, mat, moan
15 **s** shall, seal, small, snail

16 **trout**	17 **noise**
18 **thick**	19 **plate**

20 **sport**

21

M	I	S	T
A	■	■	R
R	■	■	I
K	E	E	P

22

H	A	L	F
A	■	■	I
R	■	■	R
D	A	T	E

23

P	A	R	T
E	■	■	I
A	■	■	D
R	I	P	E

24 **12** The numbers increase by 3 each time.
25 **6** The numbers decrease by 2 each time.
26 **36** The numbers increase by 12 each time.
27 **54** The numbers increase by 11 each time.
28 **343** The numbers increase by 111 each time.
29–33 Three of the words begin with 'T'. Look at the beginning of the codes. Three of the codes start with '7'. Therefore, 'T' = '7'. From this information, you can deduce TO = 72. 'O' therefore = 2. So, TOO = 722. You can now work out all the other codes.
29 **722** T = 7, O = 2, O = 2
30 **247** O = 2, U = 4, T = 7
31 **727** T = 7, O = 2, T = 7
32 **72** T = 7, O = 2
33 **46** U = 4, P = 6
34 **6** 1 + 2 + 3 = 6
35 **7** 3 + (2 × 2) = 7
36 **6** (2 × 1) + (2 × 2) = 6
37 **dear** There is no 'a' in CONSIDER.
38 **flow** There is no 'f' in LOWEST.
39 **eaten** There is no 'n' in TEACHER.
40 **need** There is only one 'e' in INSIDE.
41–45 Write out the alphabet to help you. Go through each of the words in turn looking at the positioning of the letters.

41 **got**	42 **ant**
43 **cry**	44 **dint**
45 **flow**	

Paper 4 (pages 10–13)

1 The **dog** wagged her **tail** when she saw the treat.
2 My **mother** told my **sister** to finish her homework.

A2

3 I like to read a **book** before **bed**.

4 At my birthday **party** we ate ice cream and **cake**.

5 My mum takes the **bus** to her **office**.

6 seaweed   **7** sandcastle

8 workshop   **9** handshake

10 underwater

11

P	O	R	T
A	■	■	O
R	■	■	R
K	E	E	N

12

H	E	A	L
O	■	■	A
L	■	■	Z
E	A	S	Y

13 **ill** 'Healthy' is well whereas 'ill' is unwell.

14 **pupil** A 'teacher' instructs a 'pupil' so that a pupil learns.

15 **foe** A 'friend' is an ally whereas a 'foe' is an enemy.

16 **few** 'Many' is a lot of something whereas a 'few' means very little.

17 **part** 'Whole' means complete whereas 'part' is a section.

18 **FAN** infant   **19** **RAM** pram

20 **RAW** crawls   **21** **RAT** rattle

22 **AIR** highchair

23 was**p**   **24** hop**e**

25 **s**low   **26** ha**l**t

27 ra**i**n

28 **pink** 'K' is added to 'pin' to make 'pink' as 'k' has been added to 'sun' to make 'sunk'.

29 **hear** An 'eye' is used to 'see' in the same way an 'ear' is used 'hear'.

30 **lead** 'A' is added to 'led' as the third letter to make 'lead' as 'a' has been added to 'bed' as the third letter to make 'bead'.

31 **left** 'Top' is the opposite to 'bottom 'in the same way 'right' is the opposite of 'left'.

32 **think** 'Speak' means to 'talk' in the same way as 'consider' means to 'think'.

33 **bill** as 'B' is added as the first letter to 'ill' to make 'bill' as 'b' has been added as the first letter to 'ail' to make 'bail'.

34 **she** Arrange the words in a grid to make it easier to put them in the correct alphabetical order:

boy	yob	4th
but	tub	2nd
why	yhw	3rd
she	ehs	1st
sty	yts	5th

35–39 BE must be 24 as it is the only two-lettered word. As 4 = E, you know BEE = 244. From this you can deduce BEG and BIN and therefore BEGIN.

35 **24** B = 2, E = 4

36 **245** B = 2, E = 4, G = 5

37 **238** B = 2, I = 3, N = 8

38 **244** B = 2, E = 4, E = 4

39 **24538** B = 2, E = 4, G = 5, I = 3, N = 8

40 **14** (2 × 10) – (2 × 3) = 14

41 **12** (2 × 8) – (2 × 2) = 12

42–45 Use a grid to help you:

	Yellow top	Red top	Green trousers	Brown trousers
SUE	✓			✓
OMAR	✓		✓	
LEE		✓	✓	
JESS		✓		✓

42 **Sue**

43 **Lee**

44 **Omar**

45 **Jess**

Paper 5 (pages 13–16)

1 **h** harm, hand, has, hollow

2 **c** cold, chill, cloud, can

3 **d** dread, dream, dark, dome

4 **b** band, bright, bear, beach

5 **p** prim, power, pride, plant

6 **11:00** Ten minutes after 10:50 is 11:00 as there are sixty minutes in an hour.

7 **18:35** Twenty minutes added on to 18:15 is 18:35.

8 **12:10** Fifty minutes taken from 13:00 is 12:10 as there are sixty minutes in an hour.

9–12 Use grids to help you find the order.

9 **Friday**

Monday	2nd
Thursday	3rd
Wednesday	5th
Friday	1st
Tuesday	4th

10 **April**

May	5th
January	3rd
March	4th
February	2nd
April	1st

11 **dog**

giraffe	3rd
elephant	2nd
mouse	5th
horse	4th
dog	1st

12 **balloon**

plane	4th
helicopter	2nd
kite	3rd
balloon	1st
rocket	5th

13 **cold** If something is 'warm' it is reasonably hot. The nearest opposite to this is 'cold'.

14 **white** 'Black' is very dark whereas 'white' is very pale or bright.

15 **find** To 'hide' something is to obscure or hold back whereas to 'find' something is to locate or discover it.

16 **less** 'More' is an increase of something whereas 'less' is a decrease of something.

17 **last** 'First' is the initial one whereas 'last' is the final one or at the end.

18 **PART, TRAP** 19 **AGES, SAGE**
20 **LEAP, PEAL** 21 **WARD, DRAW**
22 **LATE, TALE**
23 **rod** 24 **pin**
25 **tin** 26 **cod**
27 **arm**
28 **64** 4 is multiplied by 4 to make 16, so 16 × 4 = 64
29 **48** 3 is multiplied by 4 to make 12, so 12 × 4 = 48
30 **8** 32 is divided by 2 to make 16, so 16 ÷ 2 = 8
31 **12** 55 is divided by 5 to make 11, so 60 ÷ 5 = 12
32 **45** 100 divided by 2 to make 50, so 90 ÷ 2 = 45
33–37 There is only one three-letter word so you know LOW = 147. All the other words begin with S, so you know S = 9. There is only one five-letter word so you know STOLE = 96418. From this information, you can work out all the codes.
33 **9647** S = 9, T = 6, O = 4, W = 7
34 **9147** S = 9, L = 1, O = 4, W = 7
35 **9687** S = 9, T = 6, E = 8, W = 7
36 **147** L = 1, O = 4, W = 7
37 **96418** S = 9, T = 6, O = 4, L = 1, E = 8
38 **pillow** The three words are connected with beds, as is 'pillow'.
39 **bus** The three words are all forms of transport that run on roads, as is 'bus'. (A 'train' runs on rails.)
40 **pigs** The three words are all farm animals, as are 'pigs'.
41 **coins** The three words are all physical forms of money, as are 'coins'.

42 **rug** The three words are all floor coverings, as is 'rug'.

43
T	O	O	L
E			O
A			S
R	U	S	T

44
S	A	I	L
H			E
O			A
T	O	O	K

45
L	E	S	S
I			E
S			E
T	A	N	K

Paper 6 (pages 16–19)

1 **long** 'Short' means brief and 'long' means lengthy.
2 **down** 'Up' is above and 'down' is below.
3 **old** 'Young' is youthful and 'old' is ancient.
4 **odd** 'Even' numbers are 2, 4, 6 and so on whereas 'odd' numbers are 1, 3, 5 and so on.
5 **loosen** 'Fasten' is to tighten or do up whereas 'loosen' is to open up or relax something.

6
I	R	O	N
D			O
L			O
E	V	E	N

7
W	E	N	T
A			O
N	A	I	L
T			D

8
B	A	T	H
A			A
R	E	A	R
E			E

9 **owl** Four of the words are types of bird. The letters of 'low' can be rearranged to make 'owl'.

A4

10 **snow** Four of the words are types of weather. The letters of 'owns' can be rearranged to make 'snow'.

11 **plum** Four of the words are types of fruit. The letters of 'lump' can be rearranged to make 'plum'.

12 **stew** Four of the words are foods. The letters of 'wets' can be rearranged to make 'stew'.

13 **foal** Four of the words are animals. The letters of 'loaf' can be rearranged to make 'foal'.

14 **LAID**   15 **CLAN**

16 **PAIL**   17 **WIND**

18 **SILL**

19 **tent** The pattern is to remove 'r' from the beginning of the first word and replace it with 't'.

20 **ice** The pattern is to remove the first letter of the first word.

21 **bar** The pattern is to remove the second letter of the first word – 'e'.

22 **meat** The pattern is to insert the letter 'a' after the second letter 'e'.

23 **ball** The pattern is to insert the letter 'b' at the front of the first word.

24–25 Write out the alphabet to help you. Go through each of the words in turn looking at the positioning of the letters.

24 **ace**   25 **most**

26 **RAY** brays   27 **ROW** crows

28 **OAR** roars   29 **ARK** barks

30 **RUN** grunts

31 **FEBA** R = F, E = E, A = B, L = A

32 **ABCE** L = A, A = B, T = C, E = E

33 **DEBA** H = D, E = E, A = B, L = A

34 **HER** D = H, E = E, F = R

35 **TEETH** C = T, E = E, E = E, C = T, D = H

36 **Monday**

Monday	Day before yesterday
Tuesday	Yesterday
Wednesday	Today
Thursday	Tomorrow
Friday	Day after tomorrow

37 **11** If the brother is 4, three times his age would be 12. Joshua's age is therefore 11 as he is a year short of being three times his brother's age.

38–39 If Mike has £1.20, Gita has 40p less, therefore 80p. I must have £1 as I have 20p more than Gita.

38 **80p**

39 **£1.00**

40 **yellow, purple** The other words are fruit.

41 **ring, hat** The other words are parts of the body.

42 **leaf, stem** The other words are types of flower.

43 **bat, ball** The other words are sports.

44

45

Paper 7 (pages 20–22)

1–5 Category A Animals (**ferret, rabbit**)
Category B Colours (**purple**)
Category C Birds (**swan, wren**)

6 **yes, no** 'Yes' means to agree or assent whereas 'no' means to disagree or dissent.

7 **teach, learn** 'Teach' is to impart knowledge whereas 'learn' is to gain it.

8 **less, more** 'Less' is fewer whereas 'more' is an increased amount.

9 **work, play** 'Work' is to study or labour whereas 'play' is to relax or to be at leisure.

10 **wet, dry** 'Wet' is filled with water whereas 'dry' is without water.

11 **stiff** There is only one 'f' in PROFITS.

12 **gnaw** There is no 'a' in GROWING.

13 **soars** There is only one 's' in COWARDS.

14 **gate** There is no 't' in GRAPPLE.

15 **teen** There is only one 'e' in PATIENT.

16 **ARCH**

17 **PLAN**

18 **MOSS**

19 ROSE

1	2		4?
G	A	T	E

	3	4?
T	I	M	E

1	2		4?
R	O	P	E

	3	4?
H	O	S	E

20 PEST

3	4		
T	H	I	N

1	2?	2?	
M	O	O	N

3	4
S	T	A	B

1	2?	2?	
P	E	G	S

21–25 Try each of the words in the first set of brackets. Do they make sense with any words in the second and third set of brackets? Only one combination of three words makes sense.

21 rabbit, hole, burrow
22 cold, jumper, wind
23 balloons, inflated, room
24 sent, text, phone
25 swam, lake, island
26 less   **27** hen
28 man   **29** red
30

H	O	S	T
Y			A
M			K
N	O	T	E

31

	S		A
O	P	E	N
	A		T
A	R	T	S

32 EDBA N = E, I = D, P = B, S = A
33 FCDE G = F, R = C, I = D, N = E
34 BCDF P = B, R = C, I = D, G = F
35 1523 T = 1, E = 5, A = 2, S = 3
36 6231 M = 6, A = 2, S = 3, T = 1
37 80 The numbers double each time.
38 16 The numbers decrease by 4 each time.
39 31 The numbers increase by 6 each time.
40 14 The numbers increase by 3 each time.
41 be The first letter is always 'b'. The second letter moves forward one place.
42 Maths 4 boys like Maths, which is twice the number of girls (2).
43 Art 6 girls like Art, which is three times the number of boys (2).
44 Science Only 1 girl likes Science.
45 ICT The column that has the same number (3) for both the boys and girls is ICT.

Paper 8 (pages 22–25)

1 6 1 + 2 + 3 = 6
2 15 4 + 5 + 6 = 15
3 4 (2 × 1) + 2 = 4
4 7 (2 × 2) + 3 = 7
5 7 (3 × 1) + (2 × 2) = 7
6 11 5 + 6 = 11
7 THREE
8 WOOL
9 LITTER
10 WATER
11 CHURCH
12–14 Try each of the words in the first set of brackets. Do they make sense with any words in the second and third set of brackets? Only one combination of three words makes sense.
12 hot, wanted, cold drink
13 coat, hanging, cupboard
14 dog, basket, growled
15 cross, happy 'Cross' means angry whereas 'happy' means joyful.
16 hard, soft 'Hard' means solid whereas 'soft' means spongy.
17 eat, drink 'Eat' is to consume solid food whereas 'drink' is to swallow a liquid.
18 shut, open 'Shut' means closed whereas 'open' means ajar.
19 cry, laugh To 'cry' is to express sadness whereas to 'laugh' is to express happiness.
20 CLIP

1	2		
R	A	S	H

	3	4
G	R	I	N

1	2		
C	L	A	N

	3	4
S	L	I	P

21 SHIN

		1	2
P	O	S	T

3	4	
A	R	M	Y

		1	2
P	O	S	H

3	4	
I	N	T	O

22 BLAB

1	2	
C	R	A	G

3	4	
E	W	E	S

1	2	
B	L	U	E

3	4	
A	B	L	E

23 SLAM

1	2					3	4
C	H	A	T	R	A	I	N

1	2					3	4
S	L	A	T	S	H	A	M

24 ACHE

	1	2		4			3
O	V	E	N	Y	O	U	R

	1	2		4			3
B	A	C	K	E	T	C	H

25 **sleep, sing** The other words are types of beds.

26 **cat, water** The other words all mean tiny.

27 **road, street** These words are nouns, while the others are adjectives (describing words).

28 **new, pretty** The other words are all types of clothing.

29 **sorry, old** The other words all express pleasure.

30 **D27** The letters move forwards one place. The numbers decrease by 1 each time.

31 **G17** The letters move forwards one place. The numbers decrease by 1 each time.

32 **85D** The numbers decrease by 5 each time. The letters move forwards one place.

33 **D5** The letters move forwards one place. The numbers increase by 1 each time.

34 **C4** The letters move backwards one place. The numbers increase by 1 each time.

35 The **car** was parked in the **drive**.

36 We went to **Scotland** for our **holiday**.

37 I have to eat my **supper** before I can have **pudding**.

38 The shop on my road **sells sweets**.

39 We are **selling** our house and **moving** to Wales.

40 **DEB** O = D, N = E, E = B

41 **CDFB** C = C, O = D, D = F, E = B

42 **DECB** O = D, N = E, C = C, E =B

43 **DONE** F = D, D = O, E = N, B = E

44 **DOSE** F = D, D = O, A = S, B = E

45 **SEND** A = S, B = E, E = N, F = D

Paper 9 (pages 25–27)

1 **blank, empty** Both words mean vacant.

2 **cut, slit** Both words mean a gash or a tear.

3 **dry, fine** Both words mean fair weather.

4 **hole, gap** Both words mean a break or an aperture.

5 **tired, weary** Both words mean exhausted.

6 **LOW** follow   7 **KEY** donkey

8 **INK** drink   9 **PIT** hospital

10 **ASK** basket   11 **e** gate, ends

12 **e** none, ears   13 **d** mind, dust

14 **t** bent, trim   15 **o** also, odds

16 RASH

1	2					3	4
C	L	A	N	S	T	O	P

1	2					3	4
R	A	T	S	F	I	S	H

17 SLOW

1	2					3	4
B	A	N	D	D	A	R	K

1	2					3	4
S	L	I	P	G	R	O	W

18 STOW

		1	2		3	4	
F	I	S	H	W	O	E	S

		1	2		3	4	
F	A	S	T	T	O	W	N

19 ARCH

	1	2		3	4		
S	A	L	T	S	O	O	T

	1	2		3	4		
P	A	R	T	C	H	O	P

20 STOP

1	2					3	4
B	U	S	H	P	I	N	K

1	2					3	4
S	T	E	P	S	H	O	P

21–25 Try each of the words in the first set of brackets. Do they make sense with any words in the second and third set of brackets? Only one combination of three words makes sense.

21 **lot, buy, party**

22 **dog, fiercely, burglars**

23 **bought, present, his**

24 **run, trip, knee**

25 **packed, movie, cast**

26 **641** E = 6, N = 4, D = 1

27 **163** D = 1, E = 6, W = 3

28 **WON** 3 = W, 2 = O, 4 = N

29 **WREN** 3 = W, 5 = R, 6 = E, 4 = N

30 **ONE** 2 = O, 4 = N, 6 = E

31 **9** 3 + 4 + 2 = 9   **32** **4** (2 × 1) + 2 = 4

33 **14** (2 × 3) + (2 × 4) = 14

34–37 **Southby depart 10:30** 1 hour and 30 minutes before midday is 10:30.

Eastby arrive 16:00 1 hour and 30 minutes added to 14:30 is 16:00.

Eastby arrive 17:40 1 hour and 30 minutes added to 16:10 is 17:40.

Southby depart 17:00 1 hour and 30 minutes before 18:30 is 17:00.

38–41 Use a grid to help you:

FAIRY	A	F	I	R	Y
PLACE	A	C	E	L	P
LIGHT	G	H	I	L	T
TEACH	A	C	E	H	T

38 **I**   **39** **E**

40 **I**   **41** **E**

42–45 Use a table to help you:

	Leaves & shoots	Snails & slugs	Weeds & grass	Flies & berries
Worzels	✓		✓	
Dingbats	✓	✓		
Sninks		✓		✓
Wigglers			✓	✓

42 **Sninks**   **43** **Dingbats**

44 **Sninks**   **45** **Wigglers**

Paper 10 (pages 27–30)

1 **child, parent** The other words are all connected to cleanliness.

2 **newspaper, comic** The other words are all circular objects.

3 **apple, cherry** The other words are all colours.

4 **white, brown** The other words are items of clothing.

5 **arm, leg** The other words are all pieces of furniture you sit on.

6 **AIR** chair   7 **OUR** course

8 **BEG** begins   9 **ACT** actors

10 **ROW** brown

11 **d** land, dare   12 **r** fear, rule

13 **e** gone, ever   14 **p** stop, pond

15 **w** claw, white

16–20 There is only one two-letter word so AT must be 15. There is only one four-letter word so CHAT must be 2315. HAT must be 315, as CHAT is 2315. C is therefore 2 so ACT = 125, leaving THE as 534.

16 **15**   17 **534**

18 **2315**   19 **315**

20 **125**

21 Use a grid to help you:

f	o	u	r	5th
f	o	r	k	4th
f	i	r	e	3rd
f	a	l	l	1st
f	e	e	l	2nd

21 **fork**

22 **E** CHASE in alphabetical order is ACEHS. The middle letter is 'E'.

23–27 Try each of the words in the first set of brackets. Do they make sense with any words in the second and third set of brackets? Only one combination of three words makes sense.

23 **spade, beach, castle**

24 **fixed, pipe, basin**

25 **heard, burglar, house**

26 **help, lift, table**

27 **owl, hooted, wood**

28 **w** whale, wrap, win, wart

29 **b** blame, bright, bone, burn

30 **f** flint, fray, frank, flea

31 **o** open, oat, opal, orange

32 **c** clip, climb, cheat, charm

33 **SORT**

1	2					3	4
V	E	S	T		P	A	I	N

1	2					3	4
S	O	M	E		T	A	R	T

34 **BULK**

	2	3			1			4
	H	A	R	P		P	O	R	T

	2	3			1			4
	G	U	L	P		B	A	R	K

35 **STAB**

		1	2				3	4
	M	A	S	H		T	R	I	P

		1	2				3	4
	F	I	S	T		G	R	A	B

36 **HOPE**

1	2					3	4
S	E	L	L		B	E	A	T

1	2					3	4
H	O	M	E		R	I	P	E

A8

37 EASY

	1	2				3	4
M	A	R	K	H	E	M	S

	1	2				3	4
P	E	A	L	B	U	S	Y

38 loud

40 shin

42 pan

44 tools stool

39 cub

41 lie

43 slip lips

45 toga goat

Paper 11 (pages 31–33)

1

D		L	
O	P	A	L
N		T	
E	V	E	R

2

	H		N
T	A	M	E
	T		E
U	S	E	D

3

C	A	F	E
A		I	
R	U	S	H
T		H	

4–8 Try each of the words in the first set of brackets. Do they make sense with any words in the second and third set of brackets? Only one combination of three words makes sense.

4 yawned, tired, bed

5 bike, swerved, road

6 climbed, window, castle

7 turned, lights, dark

8 danced, rhythm, music

9 hairdresser, dentist I had a toothache so my mother took me to the dentist.

10 cage, pool The swimming pool in my town has two diving boards.

11 newspaper, dictionary When I asked my mum what a word meant she told me to look it up in the dictionary.

12 rice, bread For lunch I like a cheese sandwich on brown bread and an apple.

13 candle, cake My birthday cake this year is going to be chocolate sponge.

14 KEGCK T = K, R = E, E = G, A = C, T = K

15 KGCE T = K, E = G, A = C, R = E

16 ACI P = A, A = C, N = I

17 IGCK N = I, E = G, A = C, T = K

18 TRAP K = T, E = R, C = A, A = P

19 REAP E = R, G = E, C = A, A = P

20 PART A = P, C = A, E = R, K = T

21 mist The pattern is to remove 'l' from the beginning of the first word and replace it with 'm'.

22 all The pattern is to remove the first letter from the first word.

23 rake The pattern is to remove 'b' from the beginning of the first word and replace it with 'r'.

24 boat The pattern is to add 'b' to the front of the first word.

25 burden, load Both words mean an object that is carried.

26 kind, thoughtful Both words mean considerate or caring.

27 expect, hope Both words mean suppose or anticipate.

28 little, small Both words mean tiny.

29 hide, conceal Both words mean keep away from view or cover.

30 SHE shed

31 RAN orange

32 KIN skin

33 AGE pages

34 HIT white

35 e lone, eggs

36 h bath, horn

37 k mark, knit

38 e pane, else

39 e mare, eels

40 in inside, increase, indoor, inland

41 be because, behind, beneath, become

42 sea seaside, seashell, seagull, seabed

43 out outside, outstanding, outshine, outright

44 sand sandcastle, sandpit, sandstorm, sandpaper

45 air airport, airbag, airship, aircraft

Paper 12 (pages 34–36)

1–5 Group A Tools: **axe, saw, hammer**
Group B Musical Instruments: **drum, guitar, piano**
Group C Sports or Games: **cricket, football**
Group D Vegetables: **peas, potatoes**

6 w blow, wish

7 s pass, spin

8 w show, wind

9 t must, tidy

10 f puff, feed

11 outfit

12 beside

13 farewell

14 afterwards

15 checkout

16 boy 'Boy' is the male equivalent of 'girl' as 'uncle' is the male equivalent of 'aunt'.

17 doctors 'Doctors' treat 'patients' in the same way 'teachers' teach 'pupils'.

18 calf A 'calf' is a young 'cow' as a 'puppy' is a young 'dog'.

19 sheep A 'flock' is a collective noun for a group of 'sheep' as a 'crowd' is a collective noun for a group of 'people'.

20 burrow A 'rabbit' lives in a 'burrow' as a 'pig' lives in a 'sty'.

21

S		S	
N	E	W	S
A		A	
G	O	N	E

22

	R		A
H	E	L	D
	A		D
A	P	E	S

23

C	A	S	T
H		H	
E	V	E	N
W		D	

24 G Remove A, B, C, D and E. The first letter is 'F', the second is 'G'.

25 21 There are 26 letters in the alphabet. 26 – 5 = 21

26 February 'F' is the sixth letter of the alphabet, so February.

27 December 'D' is the fourth letter of the alphabet, so December.

28 @ ÷ + W = @, A = ÷, S = +

29 × ÷ @ R = ×, A = ÷, W = @

30 – ÷ × T = –, A = ÷, R = ×

31 WAR @ = W, ÷ = A, × = R

32 STAR + = S, – = T, ÷ = A, × = R

33–35

Mr Young's age	27	30	35
Joshua's age	2	5	10

33 Mr Young's age: 30 Mr Young is 25 years older than Joshua. If Joshua is 5, Mr Young would be 30 (25 + 5).

34 Joshua's age: 2 If Mr Young was 25 when Joshua was born, two years later Joshua would be two and Mr Young, 27.

35 Joshua's age: 10 Mr Young is 25 years older than Joshua. If Mr Young is 35, Joshua will be 10 (35 – 25).

36–40 Try each of the words in the first set of brackets. Do they make sense with any words in the second and third set of brackets? Only one combination of three words makes sense.

36 race, teacher, whistle

37 birds, seed, garden

38 flowers, pot, door

39 table, forks, knives

40 cars, work, morning

41 It is too **cold** to go **outside** today.

42 The fruit **salad** was made with grapes, pear and **apple**.

43 My aunt and uncle come and spend every **Christmas holiday** with us.

44 The police officer told the man to move his **car** because it was blocking the **road**.

45 Sometimes when I look out of my **window** at night I can see the **moon**.

Paper 13 (pages 37–39)

1

S		C	
P	E	A	S
I		L	
T	I	M	E

2

	T		H
T	A	L	E
	I		R
A	L	S	O

3

G	I	R	L
A		U	
T	I	D	Y
E		E	

4 unhappy, sad Both words mean miserable.

5 sharp, pointed Both words mean having a sharp point.

6 loud, noisy Both words mean deafening.

7 cheap, inexpensive Both words mean not costing a lot.

8 terror, fear Both words mean panic.

9 sad 'Cheerful' means happy whereas 'sad' means miserable.

10 starve 'Eat' means to feed whereas 'starve' is to go without food.

11 still 'Moving' is changing position whereas being 'still' is remaining motionless.

12 dirty 'Clean' is spotless whereas 'dirty' is unwashed and unclean.

13 hinder 'Help' is to assist whereas 'hinder' is to prevent something from happening.

14 O POUND = DNOPU, so 'O' is the middle letter.

15 N TRAIN = AINRT, so 'N' is the middle letter.

16 E READS = ADERS, so 'E' is the middle letter.

17 F AFTER = AEFRT, so 'F' is the middle letter.

18 rear **19 sore**

20 late **21 tale**

22 **sing**   23 **ride**

24 **6413** N = 6, O = 4, S = 1, E = 3

25 **1563** S = 1, A = 5, N = 6, E = 3

26 **463** O = 4, N = 6, E = 3,

27 **NOON** 6 = N, 4 = O, 4 = O, 6 = N

28 **SOON** 1 = S, 4 = O, 4 = O, 6 = N

29–31 Draw a chart to help you.

1	2	3	4	5	6	7	8	9	10
21	22	23	24	25	26	27	28	29	30

11	12	13	14	15	16	17	18	19	20
31	32	33	34	35	36	37	38	39	40

Alteratively use number logic: if 1 is opposite 21, then 2 is opposite 22, and so on. Therefore to find out the 'opposite' of any number, either add or subtract 20.

29 **28** 8 + 20 = 28

30 **34** 14 + 20 = 34

31 **19** 39 – 20 = 19

32 **fear** There is no 'a' in FLOWERS.

33 **need** There is only one 'e' in WANDER.

34 **rote** There is no 'o' in CURATE.

35 **none** There is no 'o' in MEANING.

36 **star** There is no 'r' in FASTEN.

37 **hair** hairpin, hairnet, hairslide, hairdryer

38 **under** undergo, underhand, undermine, underrate

39 **ship** shipmate, shipyard, shipowner, shipshape

40 **up** uproar, upset, upright, upward

41 **cart** cartwheel, cartload, cartridge, carthorse

42–45 Use a chart to help you:

	Green door	Brown windows	Blue windows	Red door
House 1	✓		✓	
House 2	✓	✓		
House 3		✓		✓
House 4			✓	✓

42 **1**   43 **3**

44 **2**   45 **4**

Paper 14 (pages 40–42)

1 **PINK**   2 **GREY**

3 **NAVY**   4 **MAUVE**

5 **BROWN**   6 **hotplate**

7 **rainbow**   8 **toothache**

9 **football**   10 **fireplace**

11 **m̲o̲i̲st**   12 **f̲l̲ower**

13 **f̲r̲ont**   14 **t̲r̲ots**

15 **g̲r̲ound**

16 **go, come** 'Go' means to move away whereas 'come' means to move towards you.

17 **night, day** 'Night' is when it is dark whereas 'day' is when it is light.

18 **full, empty** 'Full' means replete whereas 'empty' means with nothing in it.

19 **tall, short** 'Tall' means high or lofty whereas 'short' is small or lacking in height.

20 **play, work** 'Play' is recreation whereas 'work' is labour.

21

A	■	S	■
S	E	A	T
K	■	G	■
S	P	O	T

22

■	C	■	H
H	O	P	E
■	O	■	A
S	P	A	R

23

C	H	I	P
A	■	R	■
R	O	O	T
T	■	N	■

24 **CG** Both letters move forwards one place.

25 **8H** The numbers increase by 1 each time. The letters move forwards one place.

26 **WE** The first letters move backwards one place. The second letters move forwards one place.

27 **4S** The numbers increase by 2 each time. The letters move backwards one place.

28 **JP** The first letters move forwards one place. The second letters move backwards one place.

29 **÷ % – +** T = ÷, E = %, A = –, M = +

30 **+ % ÷** M = +, E = %, T = ÷

31 **× % ÷** S = ×, E = %, T = ÷

32 **MAST** + = M, – = A, × = S, ÷ = T

33 **ARMS** – = A, @ = R, + = M, × = S

34 **d** (8 + 7) ÷ 3 = 5; 5 = d

35 **g** 2 + (9 – 3) = 8; 8 = g

36 **b** (4 × 6) ÷ 8 = 3; 3 = b

37–40 Use a chart to help you:

	Mike	Sally	Annie	Kim
Monday	✓	✓	✓	
Tuesday				
Wednesday	✓		✓	✓
Thursday		✓	✓	✓
Friday				
Saturday	✓	✗		✓

37 **none**   38 **Annie**

39 Kim **40 Thursday**

41 **tired, exhausted** Both words mean fatigued or weary.

42 **swerve, dodge** Both words mean to avoid or to run round something.

43 **mean, stingy** Both words mean miserly or penny-pinching.

44 **soldiers, troops** Both words mean military personnel.

45 **double, twice** Both words mean twofold.

Paper 15 (pages 43–45)

1 **grass, lawn** The other words are colours.

2 **wash, dry** The other words mean friend.

3 **house, cottage** The other words are fish.

4 **plate, dish** The other words are types of food.

5 **glove, hat** The other words are all worn on the foot.

6 **light**   7 **wing**   8 **cure**

9 **cat**   10 **hat**

11

S		R	
H	E	A	T
I		I	
P	O	N	Y

12

	F		A
F	E	A	R
	T		M
V	E	R	Y

13

W	I	L	L
I		A	
D	O	T	E
E		E	

14 **sip** The pattern is to remove the second letter of the first word.

15 **feat** The pattern is to insert 'e' after the first letter of the first word.

16 **wets** The pattern is to run the letters of the first word in reverse order.

17 **race** The pattern to swap over the first and third letters of the first word.

18 **flat** The pattern is to remove the letter 'i' from the first word and replace it with 'a'.

19 **6** $1 \times 2 \times 3 = 6$ 20 **7** $(2 \times 4) - 1 = 7$

21 **12** $3 \times 4 = 12$

22–26 Try each of the words in the first set of brackets. Do they make sense with any words in the second and third set of brackets? Only one combination of three words makes sense.

22 **birthday, mother, cake**

23 **eat, chips, fish**

24 **night, wet, windy**

25 **eat, cake, poisoned**

26 **people, seen, city**

27 **+ – – +** P = +, O = –, O = –, P = +

28 **÷ / × –** I = ÷, N = /, T = ×, O = –

29 **– + × ÷ – /** O = –, P = +, T = ×, I = ÷, O = –, N = /

30 **ONION** – = O, / = N, ÷ = I, – = O, / = N

31 **TINT** × = T, ÷ = I, / = N, × = T

32 **hold** 'Contain' and 'hold' both mean to have or to enclose.

33 **final** Something that is 'last' or 'final' comes at the end or the finish.

34 **rich** 'Wealthy' and 'rich' both mean affluent or well-off.

35 **stake** 'Post' and 'stake' both mean a pole or stick.

36 **near, far** 'Near' is close whereas 'far' is a long way away.

37 **save, spend** 'Save' is to keep whereas 'spend' is to use up.

38 **ugly, pretty** 'Ugly' is unattractive whereas 'pretty' is attractive.

39 **friend, enemy** A 'friend' is an ally whereas an 'enemy' is a foe.

40 **quiet, noisy** 'Quiet' is peaceful whereas 'noisy' is loud.

41 We went to the **sea** for our holiday this **year**.

42 Mike likes to go to his grandmother's **house** after **school**.

43 I forgot that **I had** checked a book out of the library.

44 It is important to look **both ways** when crossing the street.

45 I planted some **flowers** in the garden that I'd grown from **seeds**.

Paper 16 (pages 46–48)

1–5 Try each of the words in the first set of brackets. Do they make sense with any words in the second and third set of brackets? Only one combination of three words makes sense.

1 **tired, she, sit**

2 **sister, dance, boyfriend**

3 **left, purse, shop**

4 **ring, ambulance, mobile**

5 **supper, moon, sky**

6 **trees** A 'forest' is a large group of trees so it must have 'trees'.

7 **a tail** It may have all the features but all pigs have 'tails'.

8 **man** A 'husband' is a male partner so must be a 'man'.

9 **with patients** A 'nurse's' job is to look after 'patients'.

10 **roots** Unless a 'flower' is 'rooted' in the ground, it cannot live and produce seeds.

11 **December** 12 **eleven**

13 **individual** 14 **release**

15 **alabaster**

16 $+ - \times \div /$ P = +, L = −, E = ×, A = ÷, D = /

17 $\div + + - \times$ A = ÷, P = +, P = +, L = −, E = ×

18 $+ \div - \times$ P = +, A = ÷, L = −, E = ×

19 **DALE** / = D, ÷ = A, − = L, × = E

20 **DEED** / = D, × = E, × = E, / = D

21 **crate** 22 **sold** 23 **hole**

24 **hard** 25 **super**

26 **children** 'Pupils' are usually young people who learn therefore the closest here is 'children'.

27 **pens** 'Felt tips' are a type of 'pen'.

28 **noises** 'Sounds' can be loud or soft so 'noises' is the best match here.

29 **bungalow** Although some of the words can mean places to live, a 'house' is the most similar to 'bungalow'.

30 **box** Although 'suitcase' and 'crate' are also containers, they are usually used for transporting items. 'Box' is the most similar to 'chest' here as both are used for storing items.

31 **beginning, end** 'Beginning' is the start of something whereas 'end' is the finish.

32 **open, closed** 'Open' means the contents are exposed or accessible whereas 'closed' means the contents are hidden from view or shut away.

33 **high, low** 'High' is up in the air whereas 'low' is close to the ground.

34 **strong, weak** 'Strong' is healthy and sturdy whereas 'weak' is feeble.

35 **quiet, loud** 'Quiet' means making little or no sound whereas 'loud' means making a strong and invasive sound.

36 **END** friends 37 **NUT** minutes

38 **ODE** modern 39 **EAR** years

40 **WAR** reward

41–45 Write out the first six letters to help you: ABCDEF.

41 **feed** 42 **face** 43 **bead**

44 **fade** 45 **add**

Paper 17 (pages 48–50)

1 **3** The Costa Brava has 10 hours of sunshine in July whereas London has 7, so 10 − 7 = 3.

2 **41** 6 + 7 + 7 + 7 + 6 + 5 + 3 = 41 hours

3 **8** 8 + 8 + 9 + 10 + 9 + 7 + 5 = 56. 56 ÷ 7 months = 8

4 **2** The Costa del Sol has 10 hours of sunshine in May whereas the Costa Brava has 8, so 10 − 8 = 2.

5 **13** The Costa del Sol has 11 + 11 + 11 = 33 hours of sunshine. London has 7 + 7 + 6 = 20 hours of sunshine. 33 − 20 = 13 hours difference.

6 **heavy, light** 'Heavy' means weighty whereas 'light' is weightless.

7 **here, there** 'Here' means next to you whereas 'there' indicates a distance away.

8 **whisper, shout** 'Whisper' is to speak very quietly whereas 'shout' is to speak very loud.

9 **late, early** 'Late' is delayed whereas 'early' is ahead of time.

10 **glad, sad** 'Glad' is happy whereas 'sad' is miserable.

11 **ACE** raced 12 **ROT** parrot

13 **TON** buttons 14 **ROW** brown

15 **JOY** enjoys

16 **d** hand, deal 17 **e** mate, ends

18 **t** salt, two 19 **k** duck, know

20 **t** mast, track

21 **NEST**

		1	2		3	4	
H	O	M	E		A	N	T	S

		1	2		3	4	
S	A	N	E		S	T	A	Y

22 **CHIN**

		1	2		3	4	
G	R	E	Y		E	S	P	Y

		1	2		3	4	
E	A	C	H		I	N	C	H

23 **BASH**

1	2				3	4	
W	E	S	T		A	R	T	S

1	2				3	4	
B	A	T	H		S	H	E	D

24 **BEAT**

1			4			2	3	
L	A	R	K		S	I	N	G

1			4			2	3	
B	E	S	T		N	E	A	R

25 **BEST**

1	2				3	4	
F	I	R	E		S	H	O	P

1	2				3	4	
B	E	A	R		S	T	E	W

26 **help, aid** Both the words mean to lend a hand or facilitate.

27 **ruin, spoil** Both the words mean to mar or damage.

28 **angry, cross** Both the words mean enraged or annoyed.

29 **hear, listen** Both the words mean to pay attention to a sound.

30 **price, cost** Both the words mean the amount you have to pay for something.

31–35 Solve these questions by looking at the first set of three and working out how the first and last numbers have been used to arrive at the middle number. Apply this to the second set of three and see if it works. If it does, apply it to the last set.

31 **5** $3 \times 3 = 9$ and $4 \times 2 = 8$, so $5 \times 1 = 5$

32 **9** $4 + 1 = 5$ and $2 + 5 = 7$, so $6 + 3 = 9$

33 **4** $17 - 14 = 3$ and $8 - 5 = 3$, so $11 - 7 = 4$

34 **8** $9 + 3 = 12$ and $5 + 7 = 12$, so $6 + 2 = 8$

35 **3** $30 \div 5 = 6$ and $18 \div 3 = 6$, so $24 \div 8 = 3$

36 **49** $6 \times 6 = 36$ so $7 \times 7 = 49$

37 **30** 9 is three quarters of 12 in the same way 30 is three quarters of 40.

38 **28** $14 + 7 = 21$ in the same way $21 + 7 = 28$.

39 **250** $4 \times 5 = 20$ in the same way $50 \times 5 = 250$.

40 **76** $19 \times 2 = 38$ in the same way $38 \times 2 = 76$.

41 **seed** Both words mean the part of a plant that will grow into new plants.

42 **icy** Both words mean covered by frozen water.

43 **slide** Both words mean to slip on a surface.

44 **lift** Both words mean to elevate.

45 **tilt** Both words mean to slant or be at an angle.

Paper 18 (pages 51–53)

1–5 Group A Kitchen things: **whisk, scales, recipe**
Group B Languages: **Dutch, German, French**
Group C Birds: **gull, goose**
Group D Animals: **camel, lamb**

6 **ATE** water
7 **CAR** scarf
8 **ARE** share
9 **WAS** washing
10 **TEA** steal
11 **d** land, down
12 **t** feat, turn
13 **g** gong, glass
14 **p** stop, place
15 **e** rope, ear

16

E		S	
Y	E	L	L
E		O	
S	I	P	S

17

F	O	O	D
L		A	
A	C	T	S
G		S	

18 **seat** The pattern is to add 's' to the beginning of the first word.

19 **list** The pattern is to add 's' after the second letter and before the 't'.

20 **moat** The pattern is to add 'o' after the first letter and before the 'a'.

21 **heat** The pattern is to add 'e' after the first letter and before the 'a'.

22 **than** The pattern is to add 'th' to the beginning of the first word.

23 **– / ×** G = –, E = /, T = ×

24 **$ = / @ ×** B = $, L = =, E = /, A = @, T = ×

25 **= / @ + /** L = =, E = /, A = @, V = +, E = /

26 **TAG** × = T, @ = A, – = G,

27 **GATE** – = G, @ = A, × = T, / = E,

28–31 Use a grid to help you:

	Blue jeans	Red shirt	Green shirt	Black jeans
A	✓		✓	
B	✓	✓		
C		✓		✓
D			✓	✓

28 **B**　　　　29 **D**
30 **A**　　　　31 **C**

32 **bead** ABCDEF are the first six letters. 'Bead' is the only word that can be made using only these letters.

33 **E** CRIED = CDEIR. 'E' is the middle letter.

34 **K** BROKE = BEKOR. 'K' is the middle letter.

35 **S** SWEPT = EPSTW. 'S' is the middle letter.

36–40 Try each of the words in the first set of brackets. Do they make sense with any words in the second and third set of brackets? Only one combination of three words makes sense.

36 **words, spelling, school**
37 **writer, study, book**
38 **landed, broke, applause**
39 **sister, boyfriend, birthday**
40 **spent, weekend, lines**

41 **leave, depart** Both words mean to go or set off.

42 **bitter, sour** Both words mean tart or acidic.

43 **calm, peaceful** Both words mean relaxed or tranquil.

44 **sweep, brush** Both words mean to clean using a broom or brush.

45 **grateful, thankful** Both words mean full of gratitude.

Paper 19 (pages 53–56)

1 **same** Both the words mean very alike.

2 **say** Both the words mean to speak.

3 **let** Both the words mean to permit or consent to.

4 **beloved** Both the words mean adored or treasured.

5 **tree** A 'beech' is a type of 'tree'.

6 **OUR** courts

7 **RAN** warrant

8 **BAN** armbands

9 **HAD** shadow

10 **PEN** sharpen

11 **e** gate, ease

12 **t** mint, tact

13 **e** zone, etch

14 **t** bent, trim

15 **o** also, odds

16 **MV** The first letters move forwards three places and the second letters move backwards one place.

17 **8H** The numbers increase by 2 each time. The letters move forwards two places.

18 **ABD** All the letters move forwards two places.

19 **Nb** All the letters move forward one place. The first letter is always a capital (upper case) letter. The second letter is always lower case.

20 **7VU** The numbers decrease by 1 each time. Both the letters move backwards two places.

21

D	A		L	E
E			E	
A	L	A	S	
L			P	

22

P	A	I	N
I		N	
N	O	T	E
T		O	

23

S	L	O	W
I			E
T	Y	P	E
E			K

24 **CASTLE**

25 **ANYONE**

26 **PIRATE**

27 **CINEMA**

28 **SHOPPING**

29–33 The only four-lettered word, NOTE, must be 6417. All the three-lettered words begin with 'T' except POT which must, therefore, be 541. From this, you can work out the remaining codes.

29 **145**

30 **541**

31 **144**

32 **146**

33 **6417**

34–37 Try each of the words in the first set of brackets. Do they make sense with any words in the second and third set of brackets? Only one combination of three words makes sense.

34 **queen, castle, crown**

35 **clock, on time, school**

36 **winter, snow, sledging**

37 **ill, medicine, better**

38 **nap**

39 **send**

40 **poke**

41 **soil**

42 **aunt**

43 **16** $1 + 2 + 6 + 7 = 16$

44 **18** $8 + 7 + 2 + 1 = 18$

45 **28** $6 + 8 + 7 + 7 = 28$

Paper 20 (pages 57–59)

1 **D50** The letters move forward one place. The numbers increase by 5 each time.

2 **35D** The numbers increase by 2 each time. The letters move forward one place.

3 **DW** The first letters move forward one place. The second letters move backwards one place.

4 **GH** Both letters move forward two places.

5 **T** The letters move backwards one place.

6 **11** The number added increases by 1 each time: +1, +2, +3, +4

7 **32** The numbers decrease by 4 each time.

8 **20** The numbers increase by 5 each time.

9 **18** The numbers decrease by 3 each time.

10 **35** The numbers increase by 7 each time

11–15 Two of the three-letter words begin with the same letter so the missing code must be for RAN. ADD has a double 'D' so must be 266. Therefore AND = 256. As both the four-letter words begin with 'R', R = 4. Therefore RAN = 425. From this information, you can now work out the remaining letters.

11 **425**

12 **266**

13 **4275**

14 **4751**

15 **256**

16 **26** $5 + 6 + 7 + 8 = 26$

17 **13** $5 + 3 + 4 + 1 = 13$

18 **16** $7 + 2 + 4 + 3 = 16$

19 **INCH, CHIN**

20 **BRUSH, SHRUB**

21 **NEAR, EARN**

22 **CLASP, SCALP**

23 <u>feet</u>, **teeth** I ran out of toothpaste so I couldn't brush my teeth.

24 <u>pig</u>, **dog** The dog barked to be let into the house.

25 <u>reason</u>, **fault** "It isn't my fault that the window is broken!"

26 **brief, short** Both words mean small or not long.

27 **glad, happy** Both words mean pleased or joyful.

28 **yell, scream** Both words mean to shriek or cry out.

29 **talk, speak** Both words mean to tell.

30 **see, look** Both words mean to observe or watch.

31 **BAT** battled

32 **HIP** spaceship

33 **OAR** soared

34 **LOW** followed

35 **RED** scored

36 **I** hail, lean

37 **t** most, time

38 **d** paid, drip

39 **t** belt, then

40 **e** cake, even

41 **helpless**

42 **setback**

43 **matchstick**

44 **message**

45 **indoors**

EXPANDED ANSWERS

Bond Verbal Reasoning Assessment Papers 8–9 years

NOTES

21 four   fork   fire   fall   feel

If these words were placed in alphabetical order, which word would come fourth?

_____

22 If the letters in the following word are arranged in alphabetical order, which letter comes in the middle?

CHASE _____

Complete the following sentences by selecting the most sensible word from each group of words given in the brackets. Underline the words selected.

> **Example**   The (children, books, foxes) carried the (houses, <u>books</u>, steps) home from the (greengrocer, <u>library</u>, factory).

23 Mai took her (spoon, spade, hoe) to the (garden, beach, park) to build a (bridge, castle, palace).

24 The workman (knocked, fixed, tied) the (string, pipe, paper) to the (basin, cooker, table) in the bathroom.

25 No one (heard, wanted, bought) the (washing, burglar, road) enter the (kennel, fridge, house).

26 Can you (wait, hinder, help) me (empty, lift, buy) this box onto the (lawn, table, dog)?

27 The (monster, policeman, owl) (hooted, whispered, sang) in the (cupboard, hall, wood).

5

Which one letter can be added to the front of all these words to make new words?

> **Example**   <u>c</u>are   <u>c</u>at   <u>c</u>rate   <u>c</u>all

28 __hale   __rap   __in   __art

29 __lame   __right   __one   __urn

30 __lint   __ray   __rank   __lea

31 __pen   __at   __pal   __range

32 __lip   __limb   __heat   __harm

5

Look at the first group of three words. The word in the middle has been made from the other two words. Complete the second group of three words in the same way, making a new word in the middle of the group.

Example   PAIN   INTO   TOOK   ALSO   S<u>OO</u>N   ONLY

33 VEST   VEIN   PAIN   SOME   _____   TART

34 HARP   PART   PORT   GULP   _____   BARK

35 MASH   SHIP   TRIP   FIST   _____   GRAB

36 SELL   SEAT   BEAT   HOME   _____   RIPE

37 MARK   ARMS   HEMS   PEAL   _____   BUSY

5

Remove one letter from the word in capital letters to leave a new word. The meaning of the new word is given in the clue.

Example   AUNT   an insect   <u>ant</u>

38 CLOUD   not quiet   _____

39 CLUB   a baby bear   _____

40 SHINE   part of the leg _____

41 LIFE   a fib   _____

42 PANT   used for cooking _____

5

43–45 In each list of words, the letters of one word have been jumbled up. Underline it and write it correctly.

FURNITURE   PARTS OF THE BODY   ANIMALS

    piano   slip   mare

    tools   nose   frog

    table   eyes   toga

    _____   _____   _____

3

Fill in the crosswords so that all the given words are included. You have been given one letter as a clue in each crossword.

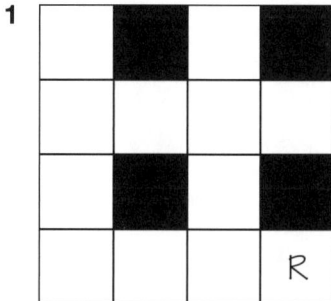

1

ever, done, opal, late

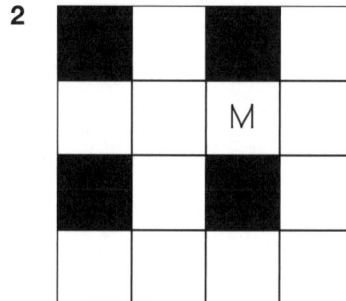

2

hats, need, tame, used

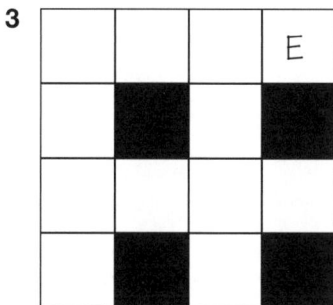

3

café, cart, fish, rush

3

Complete the following sentences by selecting the most sensible word from each group of words given in the brackets. Underline the words selected.

Example The (<u>children</u>, books, foxes) carried the (houses, <u>books</u>, steps) home from the (greengrocer, <u>library</u>, factory).

4 The old lady (smiled, yawned, laughed) because she was (tired, worried, ill) and wanted to go to (hospital, bed, play).

5 The (bike, ship, bed) (fell, swerved, ran) across the (pond, road, door).

6 He carefully (waited, cooked, climbed) through the (roof, garden, window) into the (zoo, kennel, castle).

7 She (climbed, shouted, turned) on the (lights, curtains, towels) as it was getting (light, dark, sunny).

8 Alex (hum, danced, clap) to the (rhythm, rhyme, tone) of the (music, chair, spoon).

5

Change one word so that the sentence makes sense. Underline the word you are taking out and write your new word on the line.

Example   I waited in line to buy a <u>book</u> to see the film.   _ticket_

9   I had a toothache so my mother took me to the hairdresser.   _____

10   The swimming cage in my town has two diving boards.   _____

11   When I asked my mum what a word meant she told me to look it up in the newspaper.   _____

12   For lunch I like a cheese sandwich on brown rice and an apple.   _____

13   My birthday candle this year is going to be chocolate sponge.   _____

5

If the code for PARENT is ACEGIK, what are the codes for the following words?

14   TREAT _____

15   TEAR _____

16   PAN _____

17   NEAT _____

What do these codes stand for?

18   KECA _____   19   EGCA _____   20   ACEK _____

7

Change the first word of the third pair in the same way as the other pairs to give a new word.

Example   bind, hind   bare, hare   but, _hut_

21   light, might   line, mine   list, _____

22   hair, air   hand, and   ball, _____

23   beach, reach   best, rest   bake, _____

24   oil, boil   old, bold   oat, _____

4

Underline the pair of words most similar in meaning.

Example   come, go   <u>roam, wander</u>   fear, fare

25   help, hinder   hate, horrid   burden, load

26   kind, thoughtful   come, go   top, hill

27   low, slight   expect, hope   come, depart

28   little, small   fly, down   top, bottom

29   last, ever   one, once   hide, conceal

5

Find the three-letter word which can be added to the letters in capitals to make a new word. The new word will complete the sentence sensibly.

Example   The cat sprang onto the MO.   USE

30 We keep the mower in the garden D.   _____

31 The flowers are a bright OGE colour.   _____

32 She peeled the apple and composted the S.   _____

33 Some PS of the book were torn.   _____

34 I like the yolk but not the WE of egg.   _____   5

Find the letter which will end the first word and start the second word.

Example   peac (h) o m e

35 lon (—) ggs

36 bat (—) orn

37 mar (—) nit

38 pan (—) lse

39 mar (—) els   5

Find a word that can be put in front of each of the following words to make new, compound words.

Example   cast   fall   ward   pour   _down_

40	side	crease	door	land	_____
41	cause	hind	neath	come	_____
42	side	shell	gull	bed	_____
43	side	standing	shine	right	_____
44	castle	pit	storm	paper	_____
45	port	bag	ship	craft	_____ 6

Paper 12

1–5 Look at these groups of words.

Group A Tools   Group B Musical instruments
Group C Sports or games   Group D Vegetables

Choose the correct group for each of the words below. Write in the letter.

cricket __   peas   __   axe   __   drum __   saw   __

guitar __   potatoes __   hammer __   piano __   football __

Find the letter which will end the first word and start the second word.

Example   peac (h) ome

6 blo (__) ish   **7** pas (__) pin   **8** sho (__) ind

9 mus (__) idy   **10** puf (__) eed

Underline two words, one from each group, that go together to form a new word. The word in the first group always comes first.

Example   (hand, green, for)   (light, house, sure)

11 (in, of, out)   (fit, ill, well)

12 (was, be, do)   (front, side, back)

13 (say, fare, end)   (ill, gone, well)

14 (before, when, after)   (come, wards, wet)

15 (check, pencil, pen)   (down, side, out)

Complete the following expressions by underlining the missing word.

Example   Frog is to tadpole as swan is to (duckling, baby, cygnet).

16 Aunt is to uncle as girl is to (boy, cousin, son).

17 Pupils are to teachers as patients are to (surgery, doctors, accident).

18 Dog is to puppy as cow is to (ram, lamb, calf).

19 Crowd is to people as flock is to (sheep, pigs, cows).

20 Pig is to sty as rabbit is to (drey, burrow, nest).

Fill in the crosswords so that all the given words are included. You have been given one letter as a clue in each crossword.

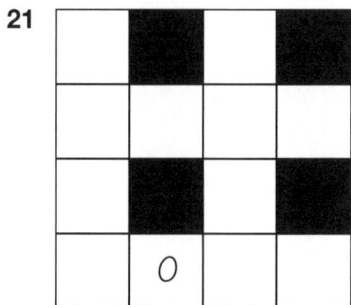

21

gone, news, snag, swan

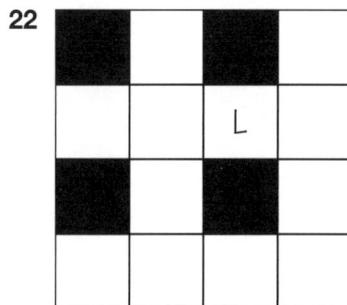

22

adds, apes, held, reap

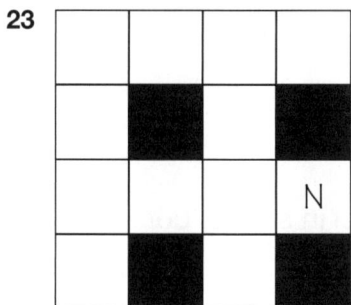

23

cast, chew, even, shed

24 If the first five letters of the alphabet were removed, which would be the second letter of those left? Circle the correct letter.

E H G F

25 How many letters would there be in this alphabet? Circle the correct number.

20 21 22

26 Which month of the year begins with the sixth letter of the usual alphabet? _____

27 Which month of the year begins with the fourth letter? _____

If the code for STRAW is $+ - \times \div$ @, what are the codes for the following words?

28 WAS _____   **29** RAW _____   **30** TAR _____

What do these codes stand for?

31 @ $\div \times$ _____   **32** $+ - \div \times$ _____

33–35 Mr Young was 25 when Joshua was born. Complete the table.

Mr Young's age	27		35
Joshua's age		5	

3

Complete the following sentences by selecting the most sensible word from each group of words given in the brackets. Underline the words selected.

Example The (children, books, foxes) carried the (houses, books, steps) home from the (greengrocer, library, factory).

36 The (race, film, job) started when the (teacher, doctor, baker) blew her (crown, pencil, whistle).

37 My mum feeds the (birds, fish, cats) each morning by putting some (jam, seed, cake) out in the (car, bin, garden).

38 In our garden we have some (swings, rocks, flowers) in a (cup, pot, dish) that sit near the back (lake, road, door).

39 Jenny set the (chair, table, television) for supper by laying out the (books, pots, forks) and (pans, knives, apples).

40 The noise of the (bikes, trees, cars) as people go to (work, sleep, play) in the (morning, holiday, sun) wakes me.

5

Find and underline the two words which need to change places for each sentence to make sense.

Example She went to <u>letter</u> the <u>write</u>.

41 It is too outside to go cold today.

42 The fruit apple was made with grapes, pear and salad.

43 My aunt and uncle come and spend every holiday Christmas with us.

44 The police officer told the man to move his road because it was blocking the car.

45 Sometimes when I look out of my moon at night I can see the window.

5

Fill in the crosswords so that all the given words are included. You have been given one letter as a clue in each crossword.

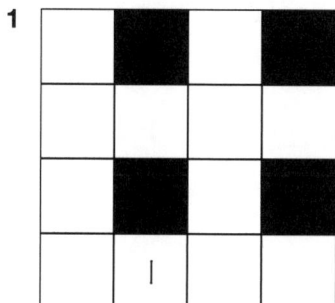

1

2

calm, peas, spit, time

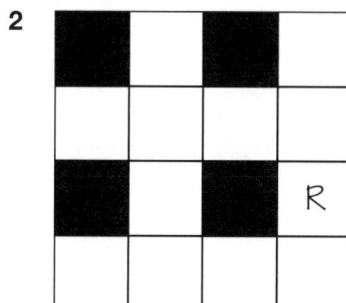

also, hero, tail, tale

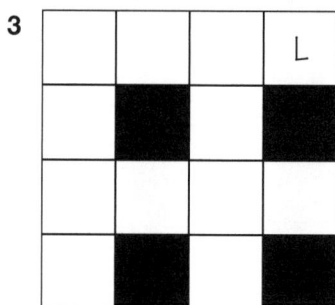

3

gate, girl, rude, tidy

3

Underline the pair of words most similar in meaning.

Example come, go   <u>roam, wander</u>   fear, fare

4 unhappy, sad   many, few   speak, listen

5 accept, refuse   divide, add   sharp, pointed

6 buy, sell   throw, catch   loud, noisy

7 cheap, inexpensive   generous, mean   rough, smooth

8 feeble, strong   give, take   terror, fear

5

Underline one word in the brackets which is most opposite in meaning to the word in capitals.

Example WIDE   (broad   vague   long   <u>narrow</u>   motorway)

9 CHEERFUL   (happy   pleased   sad   joyful   thoughtful)

10 EAT   (meals   starve   hungry   food   dine)

11	MOVING	(jump still run skip slow)
12	CLEAN	(tint washed dirty dyed spill)
13	HELP	(aid assist hinder flop earn)

5

If the letters in the following words are arranged in alphabetical order, which letter comes in the middle?

14 POUND _____

15 TRAIN _____

16 READS _____

17 AFTER _____

4

Remove one letter from the word in capital letters to leave a new word. The meaning of the new word is given in the clue.

Example AUNT an insect <u>ant</u>

18 DREAR at the back _____

19 SHORE painful _____

20 PLATE opposite of early _____

21 STALE a story _____

22 SINGE make a tune with the voice _____

23 PRIDE to go on horseback _____

6

If the code for SEASON is 135146, what are the codes for the following words?

24 NOSE _____   25 SANE _____   26 ONE _____

What do these codes stand for?

27 6446 _____   28 1446 _____

5

The pegs on one side of a cloakroom are numbered 1 to 20. On the other side they are numbered 21 to 40. 1 is opposite 21.

29 What number peg is opposite 8? ___

30 What number peg is opposite 14? ___

31 What number peg is opposite 39? ___

3

Underline the one word which **cannot be made** from the letters of the word in capital letters.

Example   STATIONERY   stone   tyres   ration   <u>nation</u>   noisy

32 FLOWERS   slow   swore   fear   wore   flow

33 WANDER   wand   dear   draw   need   read

34 CURATE   rate   cater   rote   cart   care

35 MEANING   nine   main   game   none   mane

36 FASTEN   east   seat   neat   fate   star   ◯ 5

Find a word that can be put in front of each of the following words to make new, compound words.

Example   cast   fall   ward   pour   *down*

37 pin   net   slide   dryer   _____

38 go   hand   mine   rate   _____

39 mate   yard   owner   shape   _____

40 roar   set   right   ward   _____

41 wheel   load   ridge   horse   _____   ◯ 5

Houses 1 and 2 have green doors.

Houses 2 and 3 have brown windows.

Houses 1 and 4 have blue windows.

Houses 4 and 3 have red doors.

Which house has:

   42 a green door and blue windows?   _____

   43 a red door and brown windows?   _____

   44 a green door and brown windows?   _____

   45 a red door and blue windows?   _____   ◯ 4

Now go to the Progress Chart to record your score!   Total ◯ 45

Paper 14

Rearrange the muddled letters in capitals to make proper words. They are all colours.

1 KPIN _____

2 YREG _____

3 YVAN _____

4 AEUVM _____

5 NORWB _____

5

Underline two words, one from each group, that go together to form a new word. The word in the first group always comes first.

Example (hand, <u>green</u>, for) (light, <u>house</u>, sure)

6 (old, hot, white)   (paper, plate, petal)

7 (rain, snow, wet)   (bow, arch, building)

8 (blood, tooth, pain)   (hurt, sore, ache)

9 (big, leg, foot)   (ball, park, shoe)

10 (fire, water, sea)   (switch, alarm, place)

5

Add one letter to the word in capital letters to make a new word. The meaning of the new word is given in the clue.

Example PLAN   simple   <u>plain</u>

11 MIST   to be damp   _____

12 LOWER   grows in the garden   _____

13 FONT   opposite of back   _____

14 ROTS   a horse does this   _____

15 ROUND   land   _____

5

Underline the two words, one from each group, which are the most opposite in meaning.

Exam (dawn, <u>early</u>, wake) (<u>late</u>, stop, sunrise)

16 (go, back, front)   (here, for, come)

17 (moon, night, dark)   (day, shadow, dawn)

18 (full, small, big)   (over, tiny, empty)

19 (big, height, tall)   (large, short, huge)

20 (play, lazy, good)   (hard, cross, work)

5

Fill in the crosswords so that all the given words are included. You have been given one letter as a clue in each crossword.

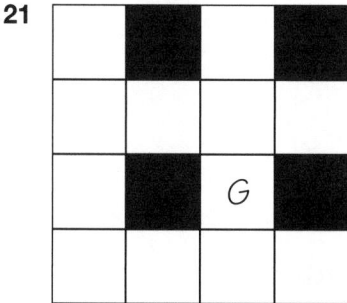

21

asks, sago, seat, spot

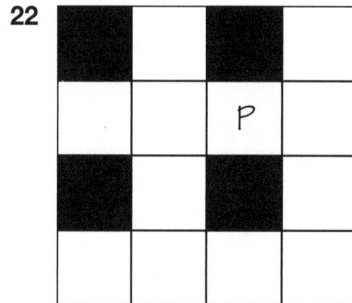

22

coop, hear, hope, spar

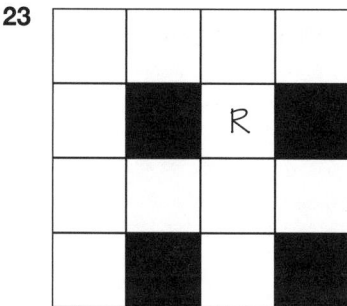

23

cart, chip, iron, root

3

Give the missing pairs of letters and numbers in the following sequences. The alphabet has been written out to help you.

A B C D E F G H I J K L M N O P Q R S T U V W X Y Z

	Example	CQ	DP	EQ	FP	_GQ_
24	AE	BF	__	DH	EI	
25	4D	5E	6F	7G	__	
26	ZB	YC	XD	__	VF	
27	2T	__	6R	8Q	10P	
28	__	KO	LN	MM	NL	

5

If the code for MASTER is + − × ÷ % @, what are the codes for the following words?

29 TEAM _____   **30** MET _____   **31** SET _____

What do these codes stand for?

32 $+ - \times \div$ _____   **33** $- @ + \times$ _____

If a = 2, b = 3, c = 4, d = 5, e = 6, f = 7, g = 8, h = 9, find the sum of these questions. Give your answers as letters.

34 $(g + f) \div b =$ _____   **35** $a + (h - b) =$ _____   **36** $c \times e \div g =$ _____

Some children do a paper round.

Mike does Wednesday and Saturday. He sometimes does Monday as well.

Sally does Monday and Thursday. She never helps on Saturday.

Annie does Monday and Wednesday. She sometimes helps on Thursday.

Kim does Thursday and Saturday. She sometimes helps on Wednesday.

37 How many of the children work on Tuesday?   _____

38 Who usually works on Wednesday but not Saturday?   _____

39 Who works on Thursday but not Monday?   _____

40 On which day of the week do Sally and Kim both work?

_____

Underline the pair of words most similar in meaning.

Example   come, go   <u>roam, wander</u>   fear, fare

41 unhappy, cross	tired, exhausted	run, skip
42 crawl, walk	sit, stand	swerve, dodge
43 mean, stingy	generous, poor	give, receive
44 army, navy	sea, harbour	soldiers, troops
45 first, last	first, tenth	double, twice

Now go to the Progress Chart to record your score!   Total   45

5

3

4

5

Paper 15

Underline the two words which are the odd ones out in the following groups of words.

Example   black   <u>king</u>   purple   green   <u>house</u>

1   green   grass   blue   lawn   red

2   wash   friend   pal   dry   mate

3   cod   house   salmon   herring   cottage

4   plate   cheese   dish   bread   butter

5   shoe   glove   boot   hat   sandal

5

Remove one letter from the word in capital letters to leave a new word. The meaning of the new word is given in the clue.

Example   AUNT   an insect   <u>ant</u>

6   FLIGHT   not heavy   _____

7   SWING   part of a bird   _____

8   CURVE   heal   _____

9   COAT   a pet   _____

10 HEAT   you wear it on your head _____

5

Fill in the crosswords so that all the given words are included. You have been given one letter as a clue in each crossword.

11

	■		■
	E		
	■		■

heat, pony, rain, ship

12

■		■	
			R
■		■	

army, fear, fete, very

43

13

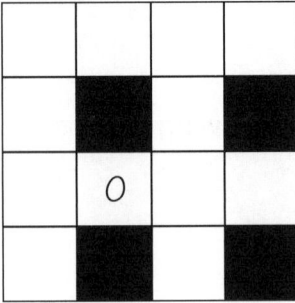

dote, late, wide, will

3

Change the first word of the third pair in the same way as the other pairs to give a new word.

    Example   bind, hind   bare, hare   but, <u>hut</u>

14 crane, cane   plot, pot   ship, _____

15 pat, peat   wed, weed   fat, _____

16 rats, star   peek, keep   stew, _____

17 lime, mile   rite, tire   care, _____

18 sit, sat   clip, clap   flit, _____

5

If a = 1, b = 2, c = 3, d = 4, find the value of the following.

19 $a \times b \times c =$ __   **20** $(b \times d) - a =$ __   **21** $c \times d =$ __

3

Complete the following sentences by selecting the most sensible word from each group of words given in the brackets. Underline the words selected.

    Example   The (<u>children</u>, books, foxes) carried the (houses, <u>books</u>, steps) home from the (greengrocer, <u>library</u>, factory).

22 On my (day, morning, birthday) my (dog, cat, mother) makes me a special (biscuit, cake, bun).

23 The girl liked to (sleep, climb, eat) (cereal, milk, chips) with her (table, soup, fish).

24 The (night, pond, moon) was (wet, slow, heavy) and (sunny, dry, windy).

25 Don't (burn, bake, eat) the (stone, king, cake). It's been (baked, poisoned, lost)!

26 Few (sheep, goats, people) have ever (seen, grazed, stolen) the ruined (hedge, pond, city).

5

If the code for POTION is $+ - \times \div - /$, what are the codes for the following words?

27 POOP _____   28 INTO _____   29 OPTION _____

What do these codes stand for?

30 $- / \div - /$ _____   31 $\times \div / \times$ _____   ◯ 5

Underline the word in brackets closest in meaning to the word in capitals.

Example UNHAPPY (unkind death laughter <u>sad</u> friendly)

32 CONTAIN   (order help hold drop box)

33 LAST   (first final try start ending)

34 WEALTHY   (poor money banker rich cheque)

35 POST   (wood stand box sign stake)   ◯ 4

Underline the two words, one from each group, which are the most opposite in meaning.

Example   (dawn, <u>early</u>, wake) (<u>late</u>, stop, sunrise)

36 (help, near, hope)   (far, away, gone)

37 (save, money, box)   (shop, keeper, spend)

38 (paint, brush, ugly)   (colour, pretty, box)

39 (pat, like, friend)   (unkind, sad, enemy)

40 (sound, quiet, song)   (noisy, voice, sang)   ◯ 5

Find and underline the two words which need to change places for each sentence to make sense.

Example   She went to <u>letter</u> the <u>write</u>.

41 We went to the year for our holiday this sea.

42 Mike likes to go to his grandmother's school after house.

43 I forgot that had I checked a book out of the library.

44 It is important to look ways both when crossing the street.

45 I planted some seeds in the garden that I'd grown from flowers.   ◯ 5

Paper 16

Complete the following sentences by selecting the most sensible word from each group of words given in the brackets. Underline the words selected.

Example   The (<u>children</u>, books, foxes) carried the (houses, <u>books</u>, steps) home from the (greengrocer, <u>library</u>, factory).

1 She was very (cross, tired, glad) and said (she, he, it) would like to (stand, sit, run) down.

2 My older (mother, aunt, sister) went to a (school, dance, bag) with her (suitcase, dog, boyfriend).

3 She (left, gave, ate) her (car, pancake, purse) in the (pond, sea, shop).

4 Can you (speak, tell, ring) for the (ambulance, trolley, driving) from your (free, mobile, call) phone?

5 After (breakfast, lunch, supper) the (keys, bikes, moon) came up in the (day, afternoon, sky).

5

Choose the word or phrase that makes each sentence true.

Example   A LIBRARY always has (posters, a carpet, books, DVDs, stairs).

6 A FOREST always has (benches, a lake, paths, flowers, trees).

7 A PIG always has (a name, a tag, a sty, a tail, spots).

8 A HUSBAND is always a (father, man, worker, driver, golfer).

9 A NURSE always works (alone, in a hospital, with patients, at night, in a city).

10 A FLOWER always has (a smell, thorns, roots, two leaves, yellow petals).

5

Underline any word which has the same letter three times.

11 December	Saturday	appears	potato
12 sparrow	trick	eleven	herring
13 individual	indeed	lesson	ironing
14 shines	eatable	release	gossip
15 necessary	alabaster	awkward	series

5

If the code for PLEASED is $+ - \times \div = \times /$, what are the codes for the following words?

16 PLEAD _____ **17** APPLE _____ **18** PALE _____

What do these codes stand for?

19 $/ \div - \times$ _____ **20** $/ \times \times /$ _____

5

Remove one letter from the word in capital letters to leave a new word. The meaning of the new word is given in the clue.

> **Example** AUNT an insect <u>ant</u>

21 CREATE a box _____

22 SOLID bought by someone _____

23 WHOLE an opening _____

24 HEARD not soft _____

25 SUPPER great _____

5

Underline the word in the brackets closest in meaning to the word in capitals.

> **Example** UNHAPPY (unkind death laughter <u>sad</u> friendly)

26 PUPILS (teacher parents friends children neighbours)

27 FELT TIPS (rulers writing books paper pens)

28 SOUNDS (whispers shouts silence noises cries)

29 HOUSE (office shed bungalow castle airport)

30 CHEST (arm leg box suitcase crate)

5

Underline the pair of words most opposite in meaning.

> **Example** cup, mug coffee, milk <u>hot, cold</u>

31 beginning, end unkind, stern safe, alive

32 smooth, soft open, closed first, fast

33 pick, pack high, low short, call

34 strong, weak up, above eat, food

35 sleep, tired noise, shout quiet, loud

5

Find the three-letter word which can be added to the letters in capitals to make a new word. The new word will complete the sentence sensibly.

Example The cat sprang onto the MO. <u>USE</u>

36 My FRIS are all coming to my party.   _____

37 Sixty MIES make an hour.   _____

38 The building is very new and MRN.   _____

39 We moved here three YS ago.   _____

40 The police are offering a RED of £1000.   _____ 〔5〕

In each line, underline the word that uses only the first six letters of the alphabet.

41	bake	bread	feed	abbot
42	black	face	dear	bale
43	band	aces	bead	abbey
44	fade	dream	dare	bake
45	deep	beak	bill	add

〔5〕

Now go to the Progress Chart to record your score! Total 〔45〕

Paper 17

Here is a weather chart showing hours of sunshine.

Average hours of sunshine per day

	Apr	May	Jun	July	Aug	Sept	Oct
Costa del Sol	8	10	11	11	11	9	7
Costa Brava	8	8	9	10	9	7	5
London	6	7	7	7	6	5	3

1 How many hours of sunshine should the Costa Brava have each day in July? ___

2 The Costa del Sol should get ___ hours of sunshine each day in August.

3 In July the Costa del Sol should have ___ hours of sunshine each day.

4 The Costa Brava should get ___ hours of sunshine each day in April.

5 London should get ___ hours of sunshine each day in October. 〔5〕

48

Underline the pair of words most opposite in meaning.

Example   cup, mug   coffee, milk   <u>hot, cold</u>

6 sand, beach   heavy, light   tired, sleepy

7 run, around   write, ink   here, there

8 better, best   whisper, shout   read, write

9 late, early   fish, meat   cat, dog

10 talk, speak   date, year   glad, sad   ◯ 5

Find the three-letter word which can be added to the letters in capitals to make a new word. The new word will complete the sentence sensibly.

Example   The cat sprang onto the MO.   <u>USE</u>

11 The runners RD each other to win.   _____

12 The PAR is a bird usually kept in a cage.   _____

13 'Do up the BUTS on your shirt!'   _____

14 Tim liked BN sugar on his cereal.   _____

15 Nishpa ENS the festival of Diwali.   _____   ◯ 5

Find the letter which will end the first word and start the second word.

Example   peac (h) ome

16 han (__) eal   17 mat (__) nds   18 sal (__) wo

19 duc (__) now   20 mas (__) rack   ◯ 5

Look at the first group of three words. The word in the middle has been made from the other two words. Complete the second group of three words in the same way, making a new word in the middle.

Example   PAIN   INTO   TOOK   ALSO   <u>SOON</u>   ONLY

21 HOME   MEAN   ANTS   SANE   _____   STAY

22 GREY   EYES   ESPY   EACH   _____   INCH

23 WEST   WEAR   ARTS   BATH   _____   SHED

24 LARK   LINK   SING   BEST   _____   NEAR

25 FIRE   FISH   SHOP   BEAR   _____   STEW   ◯ 5

49

Underline the two words, one from each group, which are closest in meaning.

Example (race, shop, start) (finish, begin, end)

26 (fire, help, hinder) (call, after, aid)

27 (ruin, match, result) (mend, spoil, again)

28 (hate, angry, soft) (cross, hard, fallen)

29 (talk, chat, hear) (see, listen, cost)

30 (price, garment, till) (shop, label, cost)

Find the missing number by using the two numbers outside the brackets in the same way as the others sets of numbers.

Example 2 [8] 4 3 [18] 6 5 [25] 5

31 3 [9] 3 4 [8] 2 5 [__] 1 32 4 [5] 1 2 [7] 5 6 [__] 3

33 17 [3] 14 8 [3] 5 11 [__] 7 34 9 [12] 3 5 [12] 7 6 [__] 2

35 30 [6] 5 18 [6] 3 24 [__] 8

Underline the number that completes the sentence.

36 6 is to 36 as 7 is to (49, 28, 56)

37 12 is to 9 as 40 is to (12, 20, 30)

38 14 is to 21 as 21 is to (24, 28, 32)

39 4 is to 20 as 50 is to (80, 250, 100)

40 19 is to 38 as 38 is to (19, 76, 50)

Underline the word in brackets closest in meaning to the word in capitals.

Example UNHAPPY (unkind death laughter sad friendly)

41 PIP (fruit flower seed skin flesh)

42 FROSTY (cold snowy icy bright bitter)

43 SKID (roll trip slide tumble brake)

44 RAISE (upright tall lift drop collect)

45 LEAN (tilt bend fat hungry curve)

Paper 18

1–5 Look at these groups of words.

Group A Kitchen things Group B Languages

Group C Birds Group D Animals

Choose the correct group for each of the words below. Write in the letter.

whisk ___ camel ___ Dutch ___ scales ___ gull ___

German ___ lamb ___ recipe ___ goose ___ French ___   5

Find the three-letter word which can be added to the letters in capitals to make a new word. The new word will complete the sentence sensibly.

Example The cat sprang onto the MO. U<u>SE</u>

6 Have you seen the fish in the WR? _____

7 He was wearing a stripy SF. _____

8 You must SH the money with Nina. _____

9 Put the HING out to dry on the line. _____

10 No one saw him SL the money. _____   5

Find the letter which will end the first word and start the second word.

Example peac (<u>h</u>) ome

11 lan (__) own   12 fea (__) urn   13 gon (__) lass

14 sto (__) lace   15 rop (__) ar   5

Fill in the crosswords so that all the given words are included. You have been given one letter as a clue in each crossword.

16

eyes, yell, slop, sips

17

acts, flag, food, oats   2

51

Change the first word of the third pair in the same way as the other pairs to give a new word.

Example   bind, hind   bare, hare   but, <u>hut</u>

18 and, sand   ill, sill   eat, _____

19 bet, best   cot, cost   lit, _____

20 cat, coat   bat, boat   mat, _____

21 fat, feat   mat, meat   hat, _____

22 is, this   at, that   an, _____   (5)

If the code for VEGETABLE is + / − / × @ $ = /, what are the codes for the following words?

23 GET _____   24 BLEAT _____   25 LEAVE _____

What do these codes stand for?

26 × @ − _____   27 − @ × / _____   (5)

A and B wear blue jeans. C and B wear red shirts. D and A wear green shirts. C and D wear black jeans.

28 Who wore blue jeans and a red shirt?   —

29 Who wore black jeans and a green shirt?   —

30 Who wore blue jeans and a green shirt?   —

31 Who wore black jeans and a red shirt?   —   (4)

32 In each line, underline the word that uses only the first six letters of the alphabet.

dear   cedar   bead   feast   aside   (1)

If the following letters were arranged in alphabetical order, which letter comes in the middle?

33 CRIED   _____

34 BROKE   _____

35 SWEPT   _____   (3)

Complete the following sentences by selecting the most sensible word from each group of words given in the brackets. Underline the words selected.

Example The (<u>children</u>, books, foxes) carried the (houses, <u>books</u>, steps) home from the (greengrocer, <u>library</u>, factory).

36 I studied my (words, letters, numbers) because we had a (running, art, spelling) test at (home, school, camp).

37 The (painter, butcher, writer) worked alone in her (car, study, desk) trying to finish her (poet, works, book).

38 When the plane (landed, swam, ran) we (waved, broke, dropped) into (silence, applause, cheers).

39 My (sister, brother, father) got a ring from her (cat, boyfriend, baby) for her (lunch, job, birthday).

40 The actress (found, lost, spent) the (second, weekend, years) learning her (lines, characters, costume).

⊘ 5

Underline the pair of words most similar in meaning.

Example come, go   <u>roam, wander</u>   fear, fare

41 leave, depart   run, sit   sleep, awake

42 rough, smooth   half, whole   bitter, sour

43 messy, neat   calm, peaceful   rude, polite

44 sweep, brush   loose, tight   hungry, full

45 straight, crooked   grateful, thankful   less, more

⊘ 5

Now go to the Progress Chart to record your score!   Total ⊘ 45

Paper 19

Underline the word in brackets closest in meaning to the word in capitals.

Example UNHAPPY   (unkind death laughter <u>sad</u> friendly)

1 SIMILAR   (different wrong same familiar smile)

2 TALK   (shout say whisper argue cry)

3 ALLOW   (stop   low   ask   let   all)

4 DEAR   (sweet   light   honest   dare   beloved)

5 BEECH   (sand   sea   tree   plant   branch)

Find the three-letter word which can be added to the letters in capitals to make a new word. The new word will complete the sentence sensibly.

> **Example**   The cat sprang onto the MO.   <u>USE</u>

6 The tennis CTS were fully booked.   _____

7 The police issued a WART for his arrest.   _____

8 My sister wears ARMDS for swimming.   _____

9 When the sun shines I can see my SOW.   _____

10 I need to SHAR my pencil.   _____

Find the letter which will end the first word and start the second word.

> **Example**   peac (<u>h</u>) ome

11 gat (__) ase

12 min (__) act

13 zon (__) tch

14 ben (__) rim

15 als (__) dds

Give the missing groups of letters and numbers in the following sequences. The alphabet has been written out to help you.

A B C D E F G H I J K L M N O P Q R S T U V W X Y Z

> **Example**   CQ   DP   EQ   FP   <u>GQ</u>

16 AZ   DY   GX   JW   ____

17 2B   4D   6F   ____   10J

18 ____   CDF   EFH   GHJ   IJL

19 Ma   ____   Oc   Pd   Qe

20 9ZY   8XW   ____   6TS   5RQ

5

5

5

5

Fill in the crosswords so that all the given words are included. You have been given one letter as a clue in each crossword.

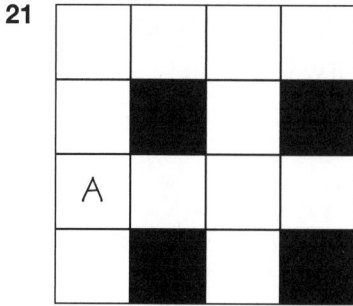

21

dale, leap, alas, deal

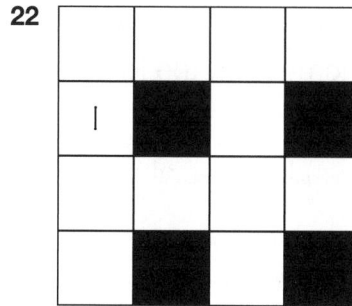

22

pain, into, note, pint

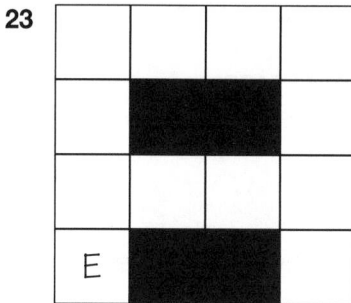

23

slow, site, week, type

3

Rearrange the muddled letters in capitals to make a proper word. The answer will complete the sentence sensibly.

Example   A BEZAR is an animal with stripes.   ZEBRA

24 We came at last to the ALECST gate.   _____

25 Has AOEYNN seen my pen?   _____

26 The IPREAT had a bag of money and a parrot.   _____

27 We're going to the NICEAM tomorrow evening.   _____

28 Please can you do the GNIPOPSH today?   _____

5

These words have been written in code, but the codes are not under the right words.

TOP	POT	TOO	TON	NOTE
6417	144	146	541	145

Write the correct code for each word.

29 TOP   30 POT   31 TOO   32 TON   33 NOTE

_____   _____   _____   _____   _____

5

Complete the following sentences by selecting the most sensible word from each group of words given in the brackets. Underline the words selected.

Example   The (<u>children</u>, books, foxes) carried the (houses, <u>books</u>, steps) home from the (greengrocer, <u>library</u>, factory).

34   The (queen, king, prince) who lived in a (shed, train, castle) only wore her (hair, shoes, crown) for special occasions.

35   I set my alarm (pen, torch, clock) for seven o'clock because I wanted to be (on time, late, known) for my first day at (school, moon, tea).

36   During the (summer, winter, autumn) we sometimes get (snow, rain, clouds) which means we get to go (sledging, eating, sun bathing).

37   When I feel (well, ill, happy) my grandmother gives me some (medicine, trousers, glasses) to help me feel (sad, worse, better).

4

Remove one letter from the word in capital letters to leave a new word. The meaning of the new word is given in the clue.

Example   AUNT   an insect   <u>ant</u>

38   SNAP   a rest   _____

39   SPEND   to tell to go   _____

40   SPOKE   to push or jab   _____

41   SPOIL   dirt or earth   _____

42   HAUNT   a relative   _____

5

If the word DAUGHTERS is written in code as 123456789, what is the sum of these words?

43   D + A + T + E = _____

44   R + E + A + D = _____

45   T + R + E + E = _____

3

Paper 20

Complete these questions. The alphabet has been given to help you.

A B C D E F G H I J K L M N O P Q R S T U V W X Y Z

Example   AB is to CD as PQ is to <u>RS</u>.

1 A35 is to B40 as C45 is to _____.

2 29A is to 31B as 33C is to _____.

3 AZ is to BY as CX is to _____.

4 AB is to CD as EF is to _____.

5 W is to V as U is to _____.   ◯ 5

Fill in the missing number in each sequence.

Example   2   4   6   8   <u>10</u>

6   1   2   4   7   __

7   40   36   __   28   24

8   5   10   15   __   25

9   24   21   __   15   12

10 7   14   21   28   __   ◯ 5

These words have been written in code, but the codes are not under the correct words. One code is missing.

RAN   ADD   RAIN   RING   AND

4751   4275   256   266

Write the correct code for each word.

11 RAN   12 ADD   13 RAIN   14 RING   15 AND

_____   _____   _____   _____   _____   ◯ 5

If the word MARIGOLD is written in code as 12345678, what is the sum of these words?

16 G + O + L + D = ____   17 G + R + I + M = ____

18 L + A + I + R = ____   ◯ 3

(57)

Underline the two words which are made from the same letters.

Example TAP PET <u>TEA</u> POT <u>EAT</u>

19 INCH CHAP CHIN NICE PACK

20 CRUSH SHUSH BRUSH SHRUB BUNCH

21 RAIN NEAT NEAR EARN TENT

22 CLASP CLASS SCORE PLACE SCALP 4

Change one word so that the sentence makes sense. Underline the word you are taking out and write your new word on the line.

Example I waited in line to buy a <u>book</u> to see the film. *ticket*

23 I ran out of toothpaste so couldn't brush my feet. _____

24 The pig barked to be let into the house. _____

25 'It isn't my reason that the window is broken!' _____ 3

Underline the pair of words most similar in meaning.

Example come, go <u>roam, wander</u> fear, fare

26 young, old brief, short good, bad

27 in, out better, worse glad, happy

28 dark, light yell, scream colour, plain

29 talk, speak cold, hot bed, time

30 read, story see, look eat, food 5

Find the three-letter word which can be added to the letters in capitals to make a new word. The new word will complete the sentence sensibly.

Example The cat sprang onto the MO. <u>USE</u>

31 We TLED through the crowds. _____

32 The SPACES landed on the moon. _____

33 The eagle SED effortlessly. _____

34 We FOLED the path to the sea. _____

35 The player SCO a goal. _____ 5

58

Find the letter which will end the first word and start the second word.

Example peac (h) ome

36 hai (—) ean   **37** mos (—) ime

38 pai (—) rip   **39** bel (—) hen

40 cak (—) ven

Underline two words, one from each group, that go together to form a new word. The word in the first group always comes first.

Example (hand, green, for)   (light, house, sure)

41 (birth, help, cradle)   (less, more, much)

42 (pick, slow, set)   (end, back, forward)

43 (in, smoke, match)   (fire, water, stick)

44 (dirty, mess, clean)   (time, old, age)

45 (let, come, in)   (room, doors, stairs)

Now go to the Progress Chart to record your score!   Total   45

Progress Chart   Verbal Reasoning 8–9 years

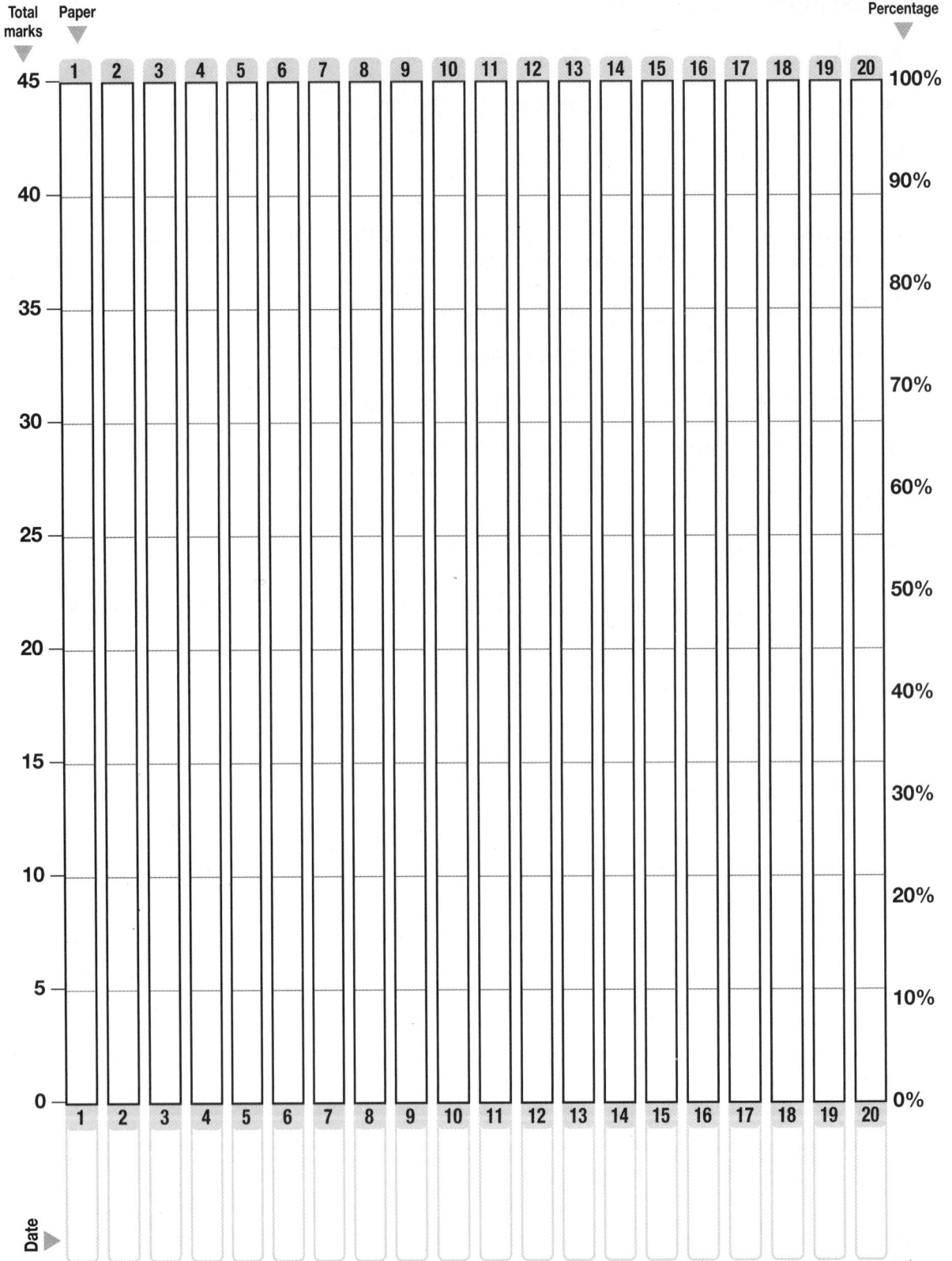

Total marks	Paper																				Percentage
45	1	2	3	4	5	6	7	8	9	10	11	12	13	14	15	16	17	18	19	20	100%
40																					90%
																					80%
35																					
																					70%
30																					
																					60%
25																					
																					50%
20																					
																					40%
15																					
																					30%
10																					20%
5																					10%
0	1	2	3	4	5	6	7	8	9	10	11	12	13	14	15	16	17	18	19	20	0%

Date ▶

When you've finished the book use the Next Steps Planner ➡